TRUE NORTH

a devotional for the real life mom

LEXI NORELL

True North: A Devotional for the Real Life Mom

ISBN: 978-0-9965215-9-8

Cover photo by Nate Norell

Hello mama,

This devotional was birthed out of my personal time with Jesus in between nap times and on the rare occasion my girls were playing together without a meltdown. This book is from my heart to yours, mama to mama. We probably don't know each other in real life, but motherhood has a funny way of bonding women without even speaking. We are part of the same tribe, and for that alone, I am so for you.

When I became a mom it didn't take me long to realize that my view of motherhood was so different than what I had expected. People around me told me I was a natural, but in reality I felt like (and often still do) a walking tornado of chaos and exhaustion. I was loving motherhood and wanting to run from it all at once, you know what I mean? This journey of raising kids, being a wife, and pursuing Jesus has been a wild one, but through it I have learned that Jesus has the deepest riches waiting for me in this season, and He is calling me nearer to Him every moment. There is honestly nothing I have ever experienced that is sweeter than knowing Jesus.

I hope this devotional takes you to the mountains, maybe not literally, but in your soul. I love the outdoors, and with the neverending noise of social media and pressures that come at us from the world, the mountains call out some kind of profound rest and wonder. Nature reminds us that before the noise, there was God. And when all the noise is gone, there will still be God. He's calling us to quiet the noise, sit with Him, know Him deeper.

As you make time between changing diapers and running those laundry loads to grow your relationship with God, know that so many are right there with you. You can do this, and I'm cheering you on from my messy living room. I have full confidence that the same God who has shown up for me will show up for you in personal and intimate ways. Praying for you, friend.

And in case you haven't been told today, you're a great mom, and God is so proud of you.

Love,

guide

TRUE NORTH IS A FOUR WEEK
DEVOTIONAL COVERING THE
TOPICS OF RELATIONSHIP, IDENTITY,
TOOLS IN MOTHERHOOD, AND
ABUNDANCE. EACH WEEK HAS
SIX DAYS THAT WILL WALK YOU
THROUGH A SHORT DEVOTIONAL,
SCRIPTURE READING, A REFLECTIVE
PRAYER, AND JOURNALING. MAKE
SURE TO CHECK OUT THE TREK
FURTHER SECTION IN THE BACK TO
DISCOVER HOW YOU CAN APPLY THE
FOCUS OF EACH DAY TO YOUR REAL
LIFE. MY HOPE IS THAT THROUGH
PERSONAL STORIES, THE WORD OF
GOD, AND TIME TO REFLECT, YOU WILL
LEAVE EACH DAY CLOSER TO JESUS.

Party of two or more? If you're
reading through this devotional
with a group of friends, then I
encourage you to go through the
"Venture On" questions and the
"Trek Further" sections together.

this is motherhood, figuring out how
to hold onto yourself while fully
giving yourself away; doing your
best while accepting your failures.
its a beautiful journey, and, make
no mistake, a messy one.

RELATIONSHIP

week one

1

TRUE NORTH

Motherhood brings unexpected trials, heaps of immense joy, and a fresh perspective on life as we know it once we become "mama." There's a whole lot of "What the flip am I doing?" and "Oh God, help me!" moments. Waves of self-doubt come flooding in, and as that tide is sucked back into the ocean, a new wave of courage and empowerment that we didn't know was in us rolls forward. This is motherhood, figuring out how to hold onto yourself while fully giving yourself away; doing your best while accepting your failures. It's a beautiful journey, and make no mistake a messy one!

Here's the deal. God has equipped and called you to be a mother. But He knows full well that without His help, it is difficult. There is so much unknown and so much wisdom that He alone holds when it comes to navigating parenthood. He calls us, now more than ever, to seek Him, hold fast to His Word, and to surrender to His will and perfect love. He has what it takes to carry you through this season of your life. It's not about gritting your teeth and pushing through it, but rather the opposite; slowing down and receiving the gifts He has waiting for you along the way. He wants to bring you through the other side fuller and more blessed and alive than when it began. God has many gifts in store for you right now. He has so many good plans for you, plans that involve redemption and grace, and being in relationship with you the way He always intended.

Weeks after my second baby girl was born, I found myself in a situation that I'm thankful no one witnessed. There I was, laying in the middle of my toddler's messy room, ugly crying, ranting out loud, "Oh God, I seriously am not cut out for this! I'm flipping tired and lonely, and just DONE. I need you!" All the while my one-and-a-half-year-old was looking at me in her Jasmine wig and saying to me, "Mama, you okay. You get better." It was a low moment. And especially not a moment I had envisioned happening while day dreaming about motherhood in my single years. I was lonely, tired, overwhelmed, and let's be honest, a bit hormonal. I realized then that while motherhood is a priceless gift, it is not for the faint of heart. I knew, more than ever, Jesus would be my greatest strength and companion on this journey. Once I got serious about seeking Him and drawing from Him like a deep and life-giving well, I began to joyfully and purposefully walk life out as a mom, wife, and friend. It's a choice to enter into the life He calls us to. Even as Christians we have to continue to choose Jesus.

Imagine motherhood like a long and rough terrain. I don't know where you are in the journey - maybe at the start, a few kids in, or you're in the stage of waiting in long school pick-up lanes, but there you are, overlooking the valleys and hills ahead of you. It's a view calling out something in your heart: desires, and passions instilled within you from creation, joined with fears and questions. And then there's Jesus, like a mountain guide with all the answers, carrying with Him the best emergency kit, tools, and snacks of course. In my imagination, Jesus looks like a wilderness dude with an Australian accent saying, "Come on you! Don't be afraid, I am the Way, I am the Truth, and I hold abundant and everlasting life. I am everything you need."

Jesus gives an abundant life! A life that promises fullness, joy, a strong confidence and assurance through all of life's valleys and hilltops. Only with Him are we safe and sound through it all. True North: the one we set our eyes on, the one who points us to the Father.

Take time to read the scriptures I've listed. Read each of them a few times, letting the truth soak in. Grab a highlighter, and as you read, highlight the promises God has made to you.

JESUS SAID TO HIM, I AM THE WAY, AND THE TRUTH,
AND THE LIFE. NO ONE COMES TO THE FATHER
EXCEPT THROUGH ME.
- JOHN 14:6 ESV -

THE THIEF COMES ONLY TO STEAL AND KILL
AND DESTROY. I CAME THAT THEY MAY HAVE LIFE
AND HAVE IT ABUNDANTLY.
- JOHN 10:10 ESV -

YOU MAKE KNOWN TO ME THE PATH OF LIFE;
IN YOUR PRESENCE THERE IS FULLNESS OF JOY;
AT YOUR RIGHT HAND ARE PLEASURES FOREVERMORE.
- PSALM 16:11 ESV -

Have you had a moment where you felt like you didn't have what it took to be a mom? Journal that moment below.

Imagine yourself and your children overlooking the mountains and valleys like on the cover of this devotional. What do you see? What fears do you have, and what are you joyfully expecting?

In what area of your life do you need Jesus to lead you today?

Prayer : Father, I thank You that we are not called to walk through motherhood alone. Thank You for being The Way, The Truth, and The Life. I don't know what will come tomorrow, but You have promised that through it all, You will be there with me. It's only in relationship with You that I find abundant life. I thank You that You have seen me through the good, the bad, and the ugly. Help me today to give You the throne of my heart, and I ask that today I would experience a renewed understanding of the unbelievable promises and faithfulness You have given to me. Give me a new perspective of what motherhood looks like as I choose to acknowledge that You are guiding me and leading me every step of the way.

- Amen

Check out the Trek Further section at the end of this book to apply today's lesson to your real life.

2

HOLY SPIRIT: OUR HELPER

One of the hardest things I ever had to admit to my husband was that I needed help. It wasn't long after we had our first little girl that I was hit in the face with the realization I couldn't do it all.

It's terrible. The moment when you finally understand you don't just suddenly gain the "mom power" hormone you thought would surge through your body once giving birth. The power to know and see all. The power to fix every problem and always know the answer. What is up with all the social media that shows women being the perfect stay-at-home moms? They always know how to make a delicious meal, they seem to have "mess free" homes, their children look well-mannered, and how on earth do they always have on clothes that look socially acceptable?

The idea I had in my mind of motherhood was far, far different than what I was experiencing.

But the truth is, and we know this by now, social media and Hollywood movies are rarely the true interpretations of real life. Are we all on the same page with that one? Good. Real life looks like late nights and early mornings, play dates, and sticky Cheerios on the floor. Real life is unpredictable. In the words of good ol' Forrest Gump, "Life is like a box of chocolates, you never know what you're gonna get." Preach it, Forrest.

The sooner we realize that we are not super-human moms, the happier and less anxious our lives will be. This isn't to say that we are totally lost. God has equipped women with part of His character and nature that really helps with the whole mothering side of things. As we get to know the Holy Spirit more, we realize that the nature of the Spirit of God reflects through women on so many levels. Nurturer, comforter, peace-keeper, counselor, these are a few of the ways Scripture describes the Spirit of God, and all of these attributes are pretty handy as a mom.

Before Jesus went to be with the Father, He said to His disciples, "It is for your benefit that I go, because if I do not go, the Helper will not come to you." How could it be for our benefit that the Son of God leave? He knew the power of the Spirit. He knew that by leaving we would be able to become homes for the Spirit to dwell in. We would receive the gift of taking Jesus with us, everywhere. His spirit *is* alive and within you. His Spirit comes to your aide in times of trouble. His Spirit is your helper, counselor, friend.

The world has offered many amazing parenting books and helpful guides, but the greatest parenting tool we could ever have is being led by the Holy Spirit. Holy Spirit cares about the little things. In decision making, when you're lost about how to discipline your children, how to be a wife and mom, ask the Holy Spirit for help. He is capable of giving direction and guidance in all areas of life, big or small.

NEVERTHELESS, I TELL YOU THE TRUTH:
IT IS TO YOUR ADVANTAGE THAT I GO
AWAY, FOR IF I DO NOT GO AWAY, THE
HELPER WILL NOT COME TO YOU. BUT IF I
GO, I WILL SEND HIM TO YOU. AND WHEN
HE COMES, HE WILL CONVICT THE WORLD
CONCERNING SIN AND RIGHTEOUSNESS
AND JUDGMENT: CONCERNING SIN,
BECAUSE THEY DO NOT BELIEVE IN ME;
CONCERNING RIGHTEOUSNESS, BECAUSE
I GO TO THE FATHER, AND YOU WILL SEE
ME NO LONGER; CONCERNING JUDGMENT,
BECAUSE THE RULER OF THIS WORLD IS
JUDGED. "I STILL HAVE MANY THINGS TO
SAY TO YOU, BUT YOU CANNOT BEAR THEM
NOW. WHEN THE SPIRIT OF TRUTH COMES,
HE WILL GUIDE YOU INTO ALL THE TRUTH,
FOR HE WILL NOT SPEAK ON HIS OWN
AUTHORITY, BUT WHATEVER HE HEARS HE
WILL SPEAK, AND HE WILL DECLARE TO YOU
THE THINGS THAT ARE TO COME. HE WILL
GLORIFY ME, FOR HE WILL TAKE WHAT IS
MINE AND DECLARE IT TO YOU. ALL THAT
THE FATHER HAS IS MINE; THEREFORE
I SAID THAT HE WILL TAKE WHAT IS MINE
AND DECLARE IT TO YOU. "A LITTLE WHILE,
AND YOU WILL SEE ME NO LONGER; AND
AGAIN A LITTLE WHILE, AND YOU WILL
SEE ME."

- JOHN 16:7-16 ESV -

BUT THE HELPER, THE HOLY SPIRIT,
WHOM THE FATHER WILL SEND IN MY
NAME, HE WILL TEACH YOU ALL THINGS
AND BRING TO YOUR REMEMBRANCE
ALL THAT I HAVE SAID TO YOU.

- JOHN 14:26 -

AND THE SPIRIT OF THE LORD SHALL REST
UPON HIM, THE SPIRIT OF WISDOM AND
UNDERSTANDING, THE SPIRIT OF COUNSEL
AND MIGHT, THE SPIRIT OF KNOWLEDGE
AND THE FEAR OF THE LORD. AND HIS
DELIGHT SHALL BE IN THE FEAR OF THE
LORD. HE SHALL NOT JUDGE BY WHAT HIS
EYES SEE, OR DECIDE DISPUTES BY WHAT
HIS EARS HEAR,

- ISAIAH 11:2-3 ESV -

In the passage
above circle every
word that is used
to describe the
Spirit of God.

In what ways is motherhood what you expected, and in what ways is it not? Journal all the things.

What are the most challenging areas of motherhood for you?

Where have you seen the Holy Spirit help you, and where do you need His guidance now?

Prayer : Father, thank You for sending Your Holy Spirit. Holy Spirit, thank You for being an everlasting and true source of help and guidance in my life. Forgive me for not recognizing the power and authority you have in my day to day, and help me to live my life through You. Help me to draw closer to You, to trust You with all areas of my life in parenting, marriage, work, and relationships.

- Amen

Check out the Trek Further section at the end of this book to apply today's lesson to your real life.

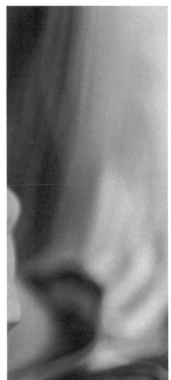

What does your day look like? If you're a mom of two toddlers like me, maybe our days look similar. Mine looks a lot like getting up with the sun, fixing bowls of cereal, fueling my veins with coffee, maybe meal planning, acknowledging and ignoring the never ending laundry pile in my room, and then remembering to put on a bra as I walk out the door. Some days are slower, and some days the hustle and bustle is on repeat. In the middle of all that life brings, how often do we stop and simply remember Jesus?

What do you turn to when the day is just too darn rough? For me, a caramel latte, hands down. Every. Time. I'm not trying to be witty, I'm just being honest. There were days when I just needed something to cope, and that was my "thing." This harmless joy in coffee eventually turned into something I needed when I felt down. "Just give me some coffee, then I'll feel better." This was my everyday mantra. I realized this pattern in my life, and knew I had to change something. Coffee isn't evil, neither is working out, watching movies, or enjoying other hobbies and activities. When good things become the *most important thing,* we need to stop and have a heart to heart with ourselves.

3

BUT FIRST, JESUS

When something or someone takes the place that is rightfully the Lord's in our life, we need to take action to place Jesus back on the throne. But first, Jesus, always.

Sometimes we fall into a rhythm that pulls us away from our joyful pursuit of our Savior and His love. The grace that was freely and joyfully given. The story that changed our destiny, forever. Have we forgotten what this is all about? The gospel. The story of God becoming fully man, through His death we gained life, a life of fullness and restoration with the Father. Before we know it, if we are not sensitive to our spirit, our tendencies turn to the world before the Creator.

Jesus came and made a way for us. He made a way to the Father that gives restoration, freedom, and wholeness. God saw the darkness that separated us from Him, and He set in motion a plan of redemption, a plan to bring us back into relationship with Him. Through the cross, through the death and resurrection of the perfect sacrifice, Jesus, we are a new creation, and Heaven is within our hearts. Through the power of the cross, Christ's death and resurrection has given us the gift of having a relationship with the Father. The cross picked us up, threw off our gunk, and His holiness, like a rushing river, came and cleansed the deepest parts within us. From the inside out we have been forgiven and made new by the power of Jesus' blood.

We must stop believing what Jesus did on the cross wasn't good enough. We must stop believing that He isn't powerful enough to restore our circumstances, heal our hearts, and renew our minds. What He has done is enough. Period.

He died for you. You were on the heart of God the day Jesus chose the cross. Jesus, being fully God, and fully man, knowing His Father's heart, saw you that day. Jesus could have called on a legion of angels as He was being beaten, tried, and crucified, but He didn't. He knew that He was the only Hope for our salvation, the only one to tear the veil and give us access to a relationship with the Father.

You are worth it. Do you believe that? It took me a long time to let that sink in. What lengths would you go to for your own child? We are only mirrors of the heart of God. How much more does he love us as His kids?

What I want you to hear today is this: because of what Jesus did on the cross, there is absolutely nothing that separates you from knowing and being loved by God. You are forgiven and made new through the love of Jesus. A child of the living God. The yucky stuff in your mind and heart, and what you hide behind closed doors, God has already paid the price for that. Turn to Him and accept the power of the cross in your life. Step into the fullness of who God is, and when the world offers other remedies to mend your heart, remember and turn first to Jesus.

Whether this is a slow day, or a crazy one, remember Jesus. And may turning to Him begin to cultivate a hunger for Him in your heart.

LOOKING TO JESUS, THE FOUNDER AND PERFECTER OF
OUR FAITH, WHO FOR THE JOY THAT WAS SET BEFORE
HIM ENDURED THE CROSS, DESPISING THE SHAME, AND IS
SEATED AT THE RIGHT HAND OF THE THRONE OF GOD.
- HEBREWS 12:2 ESV -

HE HIMSELF BORE OUR SINS IN HIS BODY ON THE TREE,
THAT WE MIGHT DIE TO SIN AND LIVE TO RIGHTEOUSNESS.
BY HIS WOUNDS YOU HAVE BEEN HEALED. FOR YOU WERE
STRAYING LIKE SHEEP, BUT HAVE NOW RETURNED TO THE
SHEPHERD AND OVERSEER OF YOUR SOULS.
- I PETER 2:24-25 ESV -

BUT HE WAS PIERCED FOR OUR TRANSGRESSIONS;
HE WAS CRUSHED FOR OUR INIQUITIES; UPON HIM WAS
THE CHASTISEMENT THAT BROUGHT US PEACE, AND WITH
HIS WOUNDS WE ARE HEALED.
- ISAIAH 53:5 ESV -

FOR GOD SO LOVED THE WORLD, THAT HE GAVE HIS ONLY
SON, THAT WHOEVER BELIEVES IN HIM SHOULD NOT
PERISH BUT HAVE ETERNAL LIFE.
- JOHN 3:16 ESV -

What is your pick me up? Do you recognize anything in your life that comes first before turning to God?

In your own words, express what the cross means to you.

Jesus died to restore our relationship with the Father. How have you seen God pursue you personally into relationship with Him?

Prayer : Father, I confess that sometimes I forget to stop and remember what You have done for me, and what You continue to do for me. Forgive me for turning to other things in times of stress or worry instead of to You. Thank You, Jesus, for the powerful sacrifice You made on the cross. Because of what You did, I can live a free and holy life in full communion with the Father. Today I want to choose You over everything else. Help me to look to You in all my times of trouble and even when things are going well. You, alone, are the only One that can satisfy my heart.

– Amen

Check out the Trek Further section at the end of this book to apply today's lesson to your real life.

4

H.O.M.E

YOU ARE BEING MADE **HOLY,**
ONE WITH CHRIST,
MADE NEW BY THE POWER OF
THE HOLY SPIRIT,
AND YOU ARE CALLED TO AN **ETERNAL**
RELATIONSHIP WITH THE FATHER.

After delivering my second baby I found myself looking in the mirror at my healing, tired body. I saw the brown line that still trailed from the bottom of my stomach up to my belly button, the empty pouch of skin that once housed my little one, and the blue, bulging blood vessels coming from my chest. I had so many feelings about my new "mom bod", and loving my body and then hating my body differed with each day. But Jesus was consistent in speaking the truth about who I was, and reminding me that I was a home for His spirit. *Me, a temple for the Holy Spirit?*

In the Old Testament, only the high priest was allowed to enter into the Holy of Holies, the place where the Spirit of God dwelled in the tabernacle. The high priest was the mediator between God and man, and he was the appointed one to bring gifts and sacrifices to God. Pretty cool job, eh? The high priest would enter into the Holy of Holies, into the dwelling place of the Spirit of God, and make a sacrifice on behalf of the people. This sacrifice was made to God as an offering to pardon the sins of the people. The protocols the priest had to do in order to be clean enough to enter that room were elaborate. It was tedious and highly thoughtful.

The Spirit of God would be upon the high priest when he would enter into the Holy of Holies. It was only the priest who could experience the glory of God, and the rest of the people could not enter into this space.

When Jesus came to earth, fully man, and fully God, there was no question that He wouldn't fulfill His purpose. He experienced the testing, emotions, and heartache that we all face. Jesus was and is the last high priest. He came as the final mediator between God and man; He came as the last sacrifice. It ended with Him. When we read in the gospels as Jesus took his final breath, it says the veil in the temple tore from top to bottom. Suddenly, there was no bearer between us and God. The Holy of Holies was open for everyone.

Jesus spoke to His disciples about the coming of the Holy Spirit before He returned to heaven. Before Christ's death the Holy Spirit would fall upon the high priest, but now we would experience Him within us. We have become the temple.

This isn't a metaphor. Jesus meant literally, that *we* would be the temple of His Spirit. Our real-life, fleshly bodies.

Take a moment to reflect on that. You, diaper-changing, house-cleaning, crazy-haired you. You are a temple for the Holy Spirit. This is your reality. This is why Jesus came. To tear the veil, to be the final sacrifice, and to make the way for us to be in relationship with God the Father.

You are not just a body. You are a temple. This is life changing. You carry the Spirit of God within you.

FOR EVERY HIGH PRIEST CHOSEN FROM AMONG MEN IS
APPOINTED TO ACT ON BEHALF OF MEN IN RELATION TO GOD,
TO OFFER GIFTS AND SACRIFICES FOR SINS.
- HEBREWS 5:1 ESV -

AND JESUS CRIED OUT AGAIN WITH A LOUD VOICE
AND YIELDED UP HIS SPIRIT. AND BEHOLD, THE CURTAIN
OF THE TEMPLE WAS TORN IN TWO, FROM TOP TO BOTTOM.
AND THE EARTH SHOOK, AND THE ROCKS WERE SPLIT.
- MATTHEW 27:50-51 ESV -

OR DO YOU NOT KNOW THAT YOUR BODY IS A TEMPLE OF
THE HOLY SPIRIT WITHIN YOU, WHOM YOU HAVE FROM GOD?
YOU ARE NOT YOUR OWN, FOR YOU WERE BOUGHT WITH
A PRICE. SO GLORIFY GOD IN YOUR BODY.
- 1 CORINTHIANS 6:19-20 ESV -

DO YOU NOT KNOW THAT YOU ARE GOD'S TEMPLE
AND THAT GOD'S SPIRIT DWELLS IN YOU?
- 1 CORINTHIANS 3:16 ESV -

GAME. CHANGER. When the reality that God's presence is encompassing all that is within us, our perspective and how we approach life will begin to change. The power of Christ is within you, and through Him your whole world is being redeemed.

When you look at your body, what feelings and thoughts bubble up?

_____

_____

_____

_____

In your own words, what are the scriptures in Corinthians speaking to you?

_____

_____

_____

_____

How does seeing yourself as a home for the Spirit of God change the way you live?

_____

_____

_____

_____

Prayer : Father, What an amazing thing You have done! You have torn the veil that separated us, and now I can be in full relationship with You. I believe that because Jesus was the perfect and final sacrifice for my sins that I have been restored and made clean, and Your Spirit lives within me. Help me to be more aware of this reality. Help me to live each day in full assurance of Your presence within my life, and show me how to steward the body You have given me.

- Amen

Check out the Trek Further section at the end of this book to apply today's lesson to your real life.

5

BAPTIZED WITH CHRIST

Both of my pregnancies were great. I didn't have any complications. I ate literally everything I craved. And besides the occasional morning nausea, I felt pretty darn good. This isn't the case for most people, so I knew better than to take it for granted.

When it came time for labor, my body decided that although pregnancy was a walk in the park, labor would be, well, labor. Both of my deliveries with my girls were long and came with different complications. Pushing out a baby just isn't my thing. Anyone else? After delivering my first, it suddenly occurred to me why they call it labor. It took work, sweat, and tears to bring a precious life into the world, and God spoke to me on so many levels throughout that process.

Despite the pain of birth, my heart was totally on fire for the precious life I had gained. My heart expanded to new heights and depths, and made large rooms full of love for each of my daughters. I didn't forget the pain, but I finally understood the love that is unshakable and unchangeable that the Father has for us. I saw a glimpse of God's heart towards us, why he would choose to go to the cross for you and me. God's heart is so much bigger and purer towards us than our hearts ever will be towards our own children, and that blows my mind.

Jesus endured the pain of death so we could have life. He took on the labor, the hours of physical and emotional distress so that we, moms like us, could experience an eternal life with the Father.

Jesus shared with us in His Word about the power of baptism. Phrases like, "new life," "born again," "raised with Christ," are all used to describe what happened in our spirits when Jesus defeated death. Through the sacrifice of Jesus, we share in His death and resurrection. Therefore, when we choose to be in relationship with Jesus we are made new through His sacrifice on the cross. With the power of Christ we can begin to break sinful habits, be healed from our past, and walk in holiness. We don't have to be governed by our sinful nature, but by the love of our Father. We are called to be children of God, pure and whole through the labor of our Savior's grace. The beauty of baptism is the power of our Spirits being made new every day through Jesus. The cross has been done, the labor is over, the life you live is under the covering of perfect love.

WHAT SHALL WE SAY THEN? ARE WE TO CONTINUE IN SIN THAT GRACE MAY ABOUND? BY NO MEANS! HOW CAN WE WHO DIED TO SIN STILL LIVE IN IT? DO YOU NOT KNOW THAT ALL OF US WHO HAVE BEEN BAPTIZED INTO CHRIST JESUS WERE BAPTIZED INTO HIS DEATH? WE WERE BURIED THEREFORE WITH HIM BY BAPTISM INTO DEATH, IN ORDER THAT, JUST AS CHRIST WAS RAISED FROM THE DEAD BY THE GLORY OF THE FATHER, WE TOO MIGHT WALK IN NEWNESS OF LIFE.

FOR IF WE HAVE BEEN UNITED WITH HIM IN A DEATH LIKE HIS, WE SHALL CERTAINLY BE UNITED WITH HIM IN A RESURRECTION LIKE HIS. WE KNOW THAT OUR OLD SELF WAS CRUCIFIED WITH HIM IN ORDER THAT THE BODY OF SIN MIGHT BE BROUGHT TO NOTHING, SO THAT WE WOULD NO LONGER BE ENSLAVED TO SIN. FOR ONE WHO HAS DIED HAS BEEN SET FREE FROM SIN. NOW IF WE HAVE DIED WITH CHRIST, WE BELIEVE THAT WE WILL ALSO LIVE WITH HIM. WE KNOW THAT CHRIST, BEING RAISED FROM THE DEAD, WILL NEVER DIE AGAIN; DEATH NO LONGER HAS DOMINION OVER HIM. FOR THE DEATH HE DIED HE DIED TO SIN, ONCE FOR ALL, BUT THE LIFE HE LIVES HE LIVES TO GOD. SO YOU ALSO MUST CONSIDER YOURSELVES DEAD TO SIN AND ALIVE TO GOD IN CHRIST JESUS.

LET NOT SIN THEREFORE REIGN IN YOUR MORTAL BODY, TO MAKE YOU OBEY ITS PASSIONS. DO NOT PRESENT YOUR MEMBERS TO SIN AS INSTRUMENTS FOR UNRIGHTEOUSNESS, BUT PRESENT YOURSELVES TO GOD AS THOSE WHO HAVE BEEN BROUGHT FROM DEATH TO LIFE, AND YOUR MEMBERS TO GOD AS INSTRUMENTS FOR RIGHTEOUSNESS.

FOR SIN WILL HAVE NO DOMINION OVER YOU, SINCE YOU ARE NOT UNDER LAW BUT UNDER GRACE.

- ROMANS 6:1-14 ESV -

There is so much to unpack from the passage. In the last verse it says that we are no longer under the law but under grace. Wow! We have been saved from the old law, and now because of Jesus, we can live under the law of grace.

Take a minute to remember how the process of becoming a mom was for you? What was laborious for you emotionally, physically, or spiritually?

Is there an area of sin in your life that God is prompting you to bring under His grace and begin walking with Him towards freedom?

What does the baptism, death, and resurrection of Christ mean for you today?

P r a y e r : Father, Thank You for taking on all the physical and emotional pain that it took for us to be together. What You did on the cross changed my whole life. Thank You that because of Your baptism, death, and resurrection, I too was baptized, died, and was risen with You. Father, forgive me for the areas of my life that are not in line with my new life in You. Forgive me for sinning against You. Help me to move forward walking in the reality that I have been risen with Christ! My life is Yours, and help me to live in a way that is in step with Your Word.

- Amen

Check out the Trek Further section at the end of this book to apply today's lesson to your real life.

6

JESUS TODAY AND ALWAYS

If I can accomplish getting myself and my children dressed, all of us fed, and drink my coffee before it goes cold, I feel like I can label that day as a success. Can I get an amen? Life is...messy. Life is...often chaotic. Life becomes...as inconsistent as a toddler's eating habits.

Being a mom can often feel like time just isn't on your side. Who has time to take care of kids, keep up with the house work, pursue a relationship with your spouse, take care of yourself, and have a relationship with God?

Too many times our relationship with God comes last. Everything else is too urgent and time sensitive. Mamas around the world, a full agenda can't replace God. No matter what it is, God deserves the throne in our lives. I say this, not to bring guilt, but to bring purpose back into your heart, and to remind you of the reason you were created-- your ultimate destiny.

You were created for one beautiful purpose: To be in relationship with Jesus. God is already complete, Holy, fulfilled, and perfect without you. For a lack of better

words, He doesn't need you, He desires you. The Trinity, in their perfect union created us as an act of love. Not to meet a need, not to gain something, but to give something. In response to the perfect love, glory, and union that the Trinity has, we were created to share in that perfect relationship.

This is your purpose. This is your destiny. What you do for God can only be in response to the love you have for Him. Love ushers in actions like worship, service, giving, and other forms of expression.

Today, while you raise kids, while you tidy the living room for the hundredth time, you are still called to relationship with God. Stretch your ears (in this case your eyes) really wide and hear what I'm about to say. You were not solely created to be a mom, or a wife, a worshiper, a missionary, (you fill in the blank). You were made to be a child of the living God. Nothing else defines you, but rather it is a gift from God, and an opportunity to expand the perfect love you have with Christ. Every good gift comes from God, and all of His gifts are an overflow of His love.

AFTER JESUS PRAYED FOR HIS DISCIPLES, HE PRAYED THIS
PRAYER OVER YOU, FOR ALL FUTURE BELIEVERS. "I DO NOT ASK
FOR THESE ONLY, BUT ALSO FOR THOSE WHO WILL BELIEVE IN ME
THROUGH THEIR WORD, THAT THEY MAY ALL BE ONE, JUST AS YOU,
FATHER, ARE IN ME, AND I IN YOU, THAT THEY ALSO MAY BE IN
US, SO THAT THE WORLD MAY BELIEVE THAT YOU HAVE SENT ME.
THE GLORY THAT YOU HAVE GIVEN ME I HAVE GIVEN TO THEM, THAT
THEY MAY BE ONE EVEN AS WE ARE ONE, I IN THEM AND YOU IN ME,
THAT THEY MAY BECOME PERFECTLY ONE, SO THAT THE WORLD MAY
KNOW THAT YOU SENT ME AND LOVED THEM EVEN AS YOU LOVED
ME. FATHER, I DESIRE THAT THEY ALSO, WHOM YOU HAVE GIVEN ME,
MAY BE WITH ME WHERE I AM, TO SEE MY GLORY THAT YOU HAVE
GIVEN ME BECAUSE YOU LOVED ME BEFORE THE FOUNDATION OF THE
WORLD. O RIGHTEOUS FATHER, EVEN THOUGH THE WORLD DOES NOT
KNOW YOU, I KNOW YOU, AND THESE KNOW THAT YOU HAVE SENT
ME. I MADE KNOWN TO THEM YOUR NAME, AND I WILL CONTINUE TO
MAKE IT KNOWN, THAT THE LOVE WITH WHICH YOU HAVE LOVED ME
MAY BE IN THEM, AND I IN THEM."
- JOHN 17:20-26 ESV -

How would you say your relationship with God is right now?

Take a moment and ask God if there are any changes within your life that need to be made for your relationship with God to grow deeper. Are there any relationships, roles, or tasks, that have taken priority over God?

How does it make you feel that Jesus prayed this prayer in John 17 for you?

P r a y e r : Father, You desire to be one with me as You are within the Trinity. You have invited me into a relationship that is beyond anything else this world can give. Today, I want to give You the first place in my life. Sometimes other things have taken the throne in my life, but today I want to give that place back to You. Show me how to pursue You even in the middle of the craziness of life. Thank You for extending grace and patience with me. Thank You for pursuing my heart and loving me so well.

- Amen

Check out the Trek Further section at the end of this book to apply today's lesson to your real life.

You have been created for relationship with your Creator. You walk this journey of motherhood with Jesus, your True North. Because of His great love for you, through creation, death, and resurrection, you now carry the Spirit of God within you, every day deepening the richness of relationship with the Father.

HE IS,
THEREFORE
I AM

week two

7

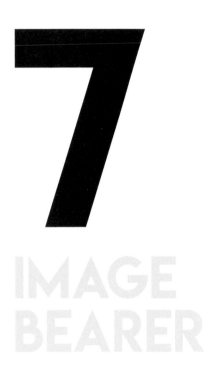

IMAGE BEARER

Life, marriage, motherhood, friendships, career paths, talk about a crazy and wild life. We become so many things during our estimated 75.2 years that it's no wonder we face an identity crisis at some point. Ever wonder what your purpose is on this planet? It's stressful to think about, right? Maybe you went to college, maybe you didn't, maybe you have always known what you're good at, and maybe you feel like you're terrible at everything. Even after getting married and having kids, I still feel like, "Ahg! What do I want to be when I grow up?!" Anyone? Isn't it a desire for all of us to come to the end of our lives and be known for something?

For too long, we have allowed the world to determine who we are and who we should be. We have given authority to things other than God to determine whether or not we are successful. Let's talk about the "mom title." Of course, you're a mom! Seriously, one of the coolest roles that you will ever have in this life (and most challenging). But, that's not the core of who you are. Who you are goes back to the foundations of who God is and who you are because of Him. He has made you in His image. It says in Genesis 1:27, "God created man in his own image, in the image of God he created him; male and female he created them." It also says at the very end of Genesis

2, that they were naked and unashamed. You see, when God created Adam and Eve, they were created in His likeness, and in God's likeness there was no shame. It isn't until chapter three that the serpent leads them into questioning their identity. Then comes shame. And it has come in all shapes and forms since that day in the Garden. In Genesis 3:10-11, because of their shame Adam and Eve hid from God, and then God asked, "who told you, you were naked?" Who told you? Friend, they never were meant to carry the weight of shame. Who told you? And I ask you the same question, who told you you were not good enough? Who told you you were someone that you were never meant to be? Who told you to question who you are?

The enemy then asked the questions we still face today, "Did God really say?" Eve was already made in the likeness of God, and the serpent tempted her by saying, "your eyes will be open and you will be like God." Eve forgot who she was. How could she, right? But how could we as well? She questioned her identity in God, took the fruit, and then knew the feeling of shame. Today this fruit that calls to us telling us we can find our true selves comes in forms of social media, magazines, and commercial ads. Did God really say you were created in His likeness? And who told you that you were naked?

God made a way through Jesus for us to live our lives back to the way He always intended: in fullness with our identity rooted in exactly who He created us to be. No shame involved. When our identity is rooted in Christ, our purpose and calling that has always been there springs forth naturally.

So, who are you? What if instead of choosing the labels ourselves, we allowed God to speak identity over our lives? He is the only one who holds the authority to call us by a name. What if we begin seeing ourselves through the eyes of the Father? What if we begin calling ourselves, "Deeply loved, full of grace, seen, confident, and redeemed?" How would that change the way we live?

Although our core identity is not in being a mother, or sister, or wife, God does assign us these roles for heavenly purposes. We are a force to be reckoned with in the kingdom of God! We will talk more about that later.

Reclaiming our true identity in Christ can sometimes take time and it takes action on our part to allow God to do His work. Read the sentences below slowly. Take it in. Maybe it feels awkward at first, maybe it will take time to renew your mind back to its original being. But that's okay.

I am made in the image of God. I resemble His beauty, His glory, and His likeness.

I am valuable and loved, not because of what I do, but because I was created, wanted, and deeply loved.

I am more than just flesh and bone. I am home to the Spirit of the living God.

Hear me when I say this: you are pretty darn cool! God has created you, and He has made you with unbelievable qualities and giftings. We should celebrate the way God has designed us. Our goal now is to refocus on the One who created us, allowing Him to restore our identity.

This week we will look at a few names we can label as truth over who we are because of who Jesus is. This is a lifelong choice we have to make, day after day allowing God to be the ultimate name giver of our lives.

DO NOT LIE TO ONE ANOTHER, SEEING THAT YOU HAVE PUT OFF THE OLD SELF WITH ITS PRACTICES AND HAVE PUT ON THE NEW SELF, WHICH IS BEING RENEWED IN KNOWLEDGE AFTER THE IMAGE OF ITS CREATOR. HERE THERE IS NOT GREEK AND JEW, CIRCUMCISED AND UNCIRCUMCISED, BARBARIAN, SCYTHIAN, SLAVE, FREE; BUT CHRIST IS ALL, AND IN ALL
- COLOSSIANS 3:9-11 ESV -

'IN HIM WE LIVE AND MOVE AND HAVE OUR BEING.'
AS EVEN SOME OF YOUR OWN POETS HAVE SAID,
'FOR WE ARE INDEED HIS OFFSPRING.'
- ACTS 17:28 ESV -

AND WE ALL, WITH UNVEILED FACE, BEHOLDING THE GLORY OF THE LORD, ARE BEING TRANSFORMED INTO THE SAME IMAGE FROM ONE DEGREE OF GLORY TO ANOTHER. FOR THIS COMES FROM THE LORD WHO IS THE SPIRIT.
- 2 CORINTHIANS 3:18 ESV -

THEREFORE, IF ANYONE IS IN CHRIST, HE IS A NEW CREATION. THE OLD HAS PASSED AWAY; BEHOLD, THE NEW HAS COME.
- 2 CORINTHIANS 5:17 -

Circle or highlight the words, "new, renewed, transformed, image, and new creation," from the scriptures above.

What titles, descriptions, and names have you allowed to define you in the past?

Take a moment to ask God what He thinks about you.

How can you apply this message to your daily life?

P r a y e r : Father, it is through You that I live, and move, and have my being. It is only through You that I discover my true identity and purpose in this life. Thank You for renewing me, transforming me, and for making me more like You. Forgive me for allowing other people or titles to define who I am when ultimately You are the only One who has the authority to do that. Help me to begin to remove all negative and untrue views of myself, and allow Your truth to seep into my very soul.

- Amen

Check out the Trek Further section at the end of this book to apply today's lesson to your real life.

SEEN

Josh and I were living in Switzerland working with a mission organization when I gave birth to our firstborn, Cora. My whole family came to visit within the first month, and I was surrounded day and night with all the help and support I could want. I was dreading the day they would all leave, and when that day came it sent me on a whirlwind of emotions. We dropped them off at the airport and I remember driving home feeling absolutely nothing, just numb. That day Josh went back to work, and as the door closed behind him, it was the first real moment I felt alone. It was just me and little Cora, and it finally hit me, the weight of responsibility, the feeling of being unqualified, and just pure terror really. *What do I do now?* The story of our relationship, mother and daughter, it was just beginning, and I felt so lonely. There were good days, and then there were bad days. Looking back, I call those first several months a fog. The good and bad days blurred together. I was exhausted and emotionally drained from trying to still be the Lexi I knew before becoming a mom, and the new Lexi who was months later still recovering from childbirth, working through the difficulties of breastfeeding, and feeling like a glorified cow. Dude, early motherhood is no joke. It was in this season that I needed to know I was seen behind those closed doors. I needed to know I wasn't alone when it was just me and my girl figuring everything out.

The one who first called God, "El Roi," which means "God who sees me," was a woman named Hagar. Throughout the whole Bible, she is the only one who calls Him by this name. I believe Hagar called God this name from a place that resonates within each of us as women. Hagar calls God by a name that speaks truth right to the core of her heart, "the God who sees me." She felt alone and hurt, and God met her where she was. I am convinced that there is something in us, within the female heart, that battles with the feeling of being hidden and unnoticed. The enemy has chosen to use this lie as a way to pierce the identity of so many of us. There are many days in motherhood that don't involve much adult interaction, and so much of what we do is done without anyone noticing. When chaos strikes, when we feel like sleep deprivation is going to kill us, when postpartum brings waves of loneliness and depression, when the mundane feels purposeless and tiring, God is with us. He sees you and He is present. In those moments that are too hard for us to handle,

we need to remember the reality of God in our lives. We have the choice to lean in and ask Him for grace and strength. Anyone been there? When it's just too much? Like Hagar, we can recognize and see that we are seen by God, and He is Emmanuel, the God who is always with us.

Back in those early motherhood days I knew in my head that God was with me, but at the same time I was experiencing loneliness. I sat around waiting for God to show up and fill the void, but it wasn't working. It wasn't until I made that first step towards God that I was so aware of His closeness. It was when I chose to turn on the water faucet that the Living Water began to pour out. God was always present, but I had to choose to enter into His presence. It wasn't until I noticed that crucial step of "knocking," of speaking out to God, of pursuing Him, that it became clear to me that access to God is always available, but I must choose to step towards Him.

And time and time again, if I give Him room, Jesus shows up for me.

I don't know your story, but I know that wherever you are today, whether it's homeschooling your kids, facing challenges in single parenting, caring for a child with disabilities, or balancing work and parenting all at once, God sees you and He is with you. You are not alone. You are known and heard and carried through it all by your heavenly Father.

SO SHE CALLED THE NAME OF THE LORD WHO SPOKE TO HER,
"YOU ARE A GOD OF SEEING," FOR SHE SAID, "TRULY HERE I HAVE SEEN
HIM WHO LOOKS AFTER ME." THEREFORE THE WELL WAS CALLED
BEER-LAHAI-ROI; IT LIES BETWEEN KADESH AND BERED.
- GENESIS 16:13-14 ESV -

FOR HIS EYES ARE ON THE WAYS OF A MAN, AND HE SEES ALL HIS STEPS
- JOB 34:21 ESV -

FOR MY EYES ARE ON ALL THEIR WAYS. THEY ARE NOT HIDDEN FROM ME,
NOR IS THEIR INIQUITY CONCEALED FROM MY EYES.
- JEREMIAH 16:17 ESV -

"BEHOLD, THE VIRGIN SHALL CONCEIVE AND BEAR A SON, AND THEY SHALL
CALL HIS NAME IMMANUEL" (WHICH MEANS, GOD WITH US).
- MATTHEW 1:23 ESV -

WHEN YOU PASS THROUGH THE WATERS, I WILL BE WITH YOU; AND THROUGH THE
RIVERS, THEY SHALL NOT OVERWHELM YOU; WHEN YOU WALK THROUGH FIRE YOU
SHALL NOT BE BURNED, AND THE FLAME SHALL NOT CONSUME YOU.
- ISAIAH 43:2 ESV -

FEAR NOT, FOR I AM WITH YOU; BE NOT DISMAYED, FOR I AM YOUR GOD;
I WILL STRENGTHEN YOU, I WILL HELP YOU, I WILL UPHOLD YOU WITH MY
RIGHTEOUS RIGHT HAND.
- ISAIAH 41:10 ESV -

GOD IS OUR REFUGE AND STRENGTH, A VERY PRESENT[B] HELP IN TROUBLE.
THEREFORE WE WILL NOT FEAR THOUGH THE EARTH GIVES WAY, THOUGH THE
MOUNTAINS BE MOVED INTO THE HEART OF THE SEA, THOUGH ITS WATERS ROAR
AND FOAM, THOUGH THE MOUNTAINS TREMBLE AT ITS SWELLING.
- PSALM 46:1-3 ESV -

Define the meaning of each name below.

El Roi

_____

_____

Emmanuel

_____

_____

What are you facing right now that causes you to need to know that God sees you and He is with you?

_____

_____

_____

How has God met you in times of loneliness?

_____

_____

_____

What is God speaking to you through this message today?

_____

_____

_____

P r a y e r : Father, I declare that You are El Roi, and Emmanuel, the God who sees me and the One who is always with me. In times when I feel unnoticed and alone, You reassure me that You have never left me. Thank You for caring so deeply about even the small things in my life. I thank You that I am made in Your image, and that part of my identity is knowing I am seen by You and walking through life in closeness with You. I pray that I would live my life in this truth, and that each day, through Your power, my mind and Spirit would be renewed.

- Amen

Check out the Trek Further section at the end of this book to apply today's lesson to your real life.

CONFIDENT

I had very different pregnancies and deliveries with both of my girls. Cora was born in Morges, Switzerland, surrounded by nurses who hardly spoke any English. One even drew a picture of my uturus to explain what was happening in my uterus because we lacked the vocabulary to talk about it. Ruby was born in Amsterdam two years later. And along with every other pregnant woman in Holland, I was riding my bike to my midwife appointment, even at 8 months pregnant, with my legs spread out as far as they could go while I pedaled down the winding streets. From language to lifestyle, culture and currency, both experiences felt unfamiliar and foreign to me.

Josh and I knew we wanted to be in full-time missions work from young ages. When we decided to move to Europe, I had so many questions about raising a family. What will healthcare be like? Is breastfeeding in public okay? What is socially acceptable? How do I sign them up for school? What if they have a hard time making friends? What American traditions do we celebrate? How will they learn a new language? How will they feel not having extended family around?

God had something to say about all this and, over time, He has been faithful to provide and care for all of the questions I started with.

Without fail, history has testified to God's faithfulness. It's another aspect of His nature that is unchanging and permanent. God's word is His word, His promises are kept, and His will will be done. Sometimes we have to let go of our own timing, our perfect plan, our expectations, and our own ideas of how things should be. We need to choose to trust that God has thought about all the details. He is faithful to guide us through the big decisions in our lives and also to provide for us in the small things.

As children of God, we can be confident that our Father in heaven is faithful to us. As we walk in obedience to His calling over our lives He is faithful to supply all we need and make a way for us.

Our confidence doesn't stem from our own strength. Our confidence comes from knowing Jesus and holding on to His promises. Christ is the Rock we rest upon, the One our salvation and hope is founded upon. Our confidence in Christ, regardless of what we feel, says, "I don't know what the future holds, but my confidence is in Jesus, and I believe what He says in His word. He will work all things together for my good." Confidence says, "I don't think I have what it takes to be a good mom and wife, but I know that God says He is with me, and He will strengthen me and help me." Through Him we look to our present and future joys and trials and we choose peace, because God is faithful in all things. We choose hope. We rest in the assurance that God will always equip us and give us the grace to walk through anything that may come. **We are confident because our God is faithful.**

It's been four years since we moved to Europe and although we face challenges, life isn't always easy and I'm still google translating every school email or doctor's report, God has shown Himself faithful through it all. He has provided community, He has blessed Cora and Ruby with sweet friends, He is making Himself known to them in intimate and beautiful ways. Even when my emotions get all up in a frenzy, my spirit can choose to rest in the assurance of God's faithfulness. No matter where we find ourselves and the questions that come, He is faithful, therefore you can live your life in confidence.

KNOW THEREFORE THAT THE LORD YOUR GOD IS GOD,
THE FAITHFUL GOD WHO KEEPS COVENANT AND STEADFAST
LOVE WITH THOSE WHO LOVE HIM AND KEEP HIS
COMMANDMENTS, TO A THOUSAND GENERATIONS.
- DEUTERONOMY 7:9 ESV -

LET US THEN WITH CONFIDENCE DRAW NEAR TO THE
THRONE OF GRACE, THAT WE MAY RECEIVE MERCY AND
FIND GRACE TO HELP IN TIME OF NEED.
- HEBREWS 4:16 ESV -

THE STEADFAST LOVE OF THE LORD NEVER CEASES;
HIS MERCIES NEVER COME TO AN END; THEY ARE NEW
EVERY MORNING; GREAT IS YOUR FAITHFULNESS.
- LAMENTATIONS 3:22-23 ESV -

IN THE FEAR OF THE LORD THERE IS STRONG
CONFIDENCE, AND HIS CHILDREN WILL HAVE A REFUGE.
- PROVERBS 14:26 ESV -

FEAR NOT, FOR I AM WITH YOU; BE NOT DISMAYED, FOR I AM YOUR
GOD; I WILL STRENGTHEN YOU, I WILL HELP YOU, I WILL UPHOLD YOU
WITH MY RIGHTEOUS RIGHT HAND.
- ISAIAH 41:10 ESV -

THE LORD IS MY LIGHT AND MY SALVATION;
WHOM SHALL I FEAR? THE LORD IS THE STRONGHOLD
OF MY LIFE; OF WHOM SHALL I BE AFRAID?
- PSALM 27:1 ESV -

Where do you need to see God's faithfulness in your life right now?

_____

_____

_____

_____

What holds you back from believing God is faithful?

_____

_____

_____

_____

How has God been faithful to you in your life?

_____

_____

_____

_____

P r a y e r : Father, I declare today that You are able and You are faithful. Forgive me for the times I have doubted Your faithfulness. Help me Holy Spirit to walk out the truth of God's faithfulness in my everyday life. Help me to not be discouraged or afraid of what I may face but, through faith expect Your faithfulness to reign over all circumstances.

– Amen

Check out the Trek Further section at the end of this book to apply today's lesson to your real life.

10
GRACE-
FULL

I hate throwup. That's my one thing when it comes to parenting I just cannot do. When I hear the dreaded "my tummy hurts" from my toddler, I just want to run and hide. Cora was two, and Ruby was only about eight months old when the stomach bug hit our home like a bomb for the first time. Josh was gone for the week, and I was home alone with the girls. I couldn't hide. I couldn't pass the puke bucket to Josh. I had to do it; there was no other option. Cora got it first, and then like clockwork Ruby and I got it. I can't describe how miserable that week was. I literally was crying all the time. I laugh a little about it now, picturing myself cleaning vomit from the carpet - in tears, missing my husband, doing the thing I never wanted to do. It was hard, and it was downright nasty, but looking back I see all the ways God provided for me during that week. First, friends showed up. One with food, one to pick me up off the bathroom floor, one to clean the dirty laundry, one to help put my kids to bed. This was my family, my kids, and vomit for crying out loud! But people showed up. God showed up. When I felt like I didn't have it in me to mother that week, God, in the late of the night, would speak to me, "I'm giving you the grace to love your children. I'm supplying the energy you need to do what needs to be done. It's not by your strength, but through mine. Here's my grace. We got this."

Grace is twofold. First, Christ came so that, by His grace, we no longer live under the law, but under grace. We can't earn it, and there's nothing we can do that qualifies us for it. Second, grace is a gift given to supernaturally equip us with what we need in order to walk through difficult trials or accomplish assignments from God. He gives us the grace we need to walk through the valleys, and climb the mountains.

When God gives us a heavenly assignment, He is faithful to supply us with the grace we need and equips us in every way to complete that assignment. Knowing that by our own efforts we will achieve some, but by yielding to God's grace and strength, we will achieve the impossible.

What mountains do you have of your own? Maybe your mountain is something God has asked you to do, and you feel like it's too big of a calling. Maybe it's pregnancy? A new job? Conflict in your marriage, a sickness or loss? Is there a mountain that feels too difficult to climb, or a valley that looks too dark to walk through?

In our weakness, Christ is strong. When we reach that point of "I can't do this!" He steps in with His supernatural grace and says, "But I can, and here's the grace I have for you to be able to do it." When we feel completely ill-equipped to do what God has called us to do, Jesus will send His grace to help us. And just as he gives His grace to us, He can fill us up with grace for others. The nights the kids just won't sleep, we're exhausted and on the verge of a meltdown, His grace can be given to us. When loving our spouse is hard, He can provide the grace you need. When work and life are just too messy and too hard, we can ask Him for His grace to extend from our lives.

Raise your hand if you need grace for yourself and for your family! That should be all of us. His grace is available for us, and His grace can overflow through us. Let's pray, and hold open our hands to receive the grace of Jesus, and then go tackle all the things that moms do.

BUT HE SAID TO ME, "MY GRACE IS SUFFICIENT FOR YOU,
FOR MY POWER IS MADE PERFECT IN WEAKNESS." THEREFORE
I WILL BOAST ALL THE MORE GLADLY OF MY WEAKNESSES,
SO THAT THE POWER OF CHRIST MAY REST UPON ME.
- 2 CORINTHIANS 12:9 ESV -

FOR SIN WILL HAVE NO DOMINION OVER YOU,
SINCE YOU ARE NOT UNDER LAW BUT UNDER GRACE.
- ROMANS 6:14 ESV -

FOR BY GRACE YOU HAVE BEEN SAVED THROUGH FAITH.
AND THIS IS NOT YOUR OWN DOING; IT IS THE GIFT OF GOD,
NOT A RESULT OF WORKS, SO THAT NO ONE MAY BOAST.
- EPHESIANS 2:8-9 ESV -

BUT IF IT IS BY GRACE, IT IS NO LONGER ON THE BASIS
OF WORKS; OTHERWISE GRACE WOULD NO LONGER BE GRACE.
- ROMANS 11:6 ESV -

BUT AS YOU EXCEL IN EVERYTHING - IN FAITH, IN SPEECH, IN
KNOWLEDGE, IN ALL EARNESTNESS, AND IN OUR LOVE FOR
YOU-SEE THAT YOU EXCEL IN THE ACT OF GRACE ALSO.
- 2 CORINTHIANS 8:7 ESV -

In your own words, describe what God's grace means to you.

_____

_____

_____

_____

In what ways have you been striving by your own strength?

_____

_____

_____

_____

Where do you need the grace of God in your life today?

_____

_____

_____

_____

Prayer : Father, thank You for Your grace. Thank You that I don't have to live on my own strength, but by Your strength. Thank You, Father, that when I face mountains in my daily life, You are there to supply what I need to climb them. I acknowledge that I can never do anything to earn or deserve Your grace, but that You give it from Your own desire. Holy Spirit help me in times of trial to lean into the grace of God. Help me to walk humbly, knowing that it is through the strength and grace of the Father that I can live this life well. I love You, Jesus.

– Amen

Check out the Trek Further section at the end of this book to apply today's lesson to your real life.

11

LOVED

Very early on when I first became a mom, I had loads of questions. Some things came naturally, but to be honest, a lot didn't. I felt the weight of responsibility and the realization that Josh and I were to cultivate a life pointing to Christ for this child of ours. Questions about feeding and nap schedules were one aspect, but what about raising spiritually healthy and God-loving kids? That was some heavy stuff. How do I raise a child with a firm identity in God? How do I know how to parent, how to raise up a child well? Why on earth isn't there a practice round? I mean, c'mon! So many people offered their best parenting book recommendations, methods, and routines they personally have done within their home. I appreciated the advice, and I knew it was all coming from a good heart, but I felt overwhelmed by it all. So many perspectives and points of view, not to mention every family and child being so different. I realized quickly that Google was my worst enemy when it came to parenting tactics. Talk about information overload.

What I know now and wish I grasped earlier, is that understanding the love of God in my personal life greatly influences the way I raise my kids. By knowing I'm loved, and loving God with all my heart in return, I become a really good mom. When we know the love that is within us, and that love is for us, and we live that love every day, it changes our perspective on parenting. It changes how we respond to our kids, how we discipline, how we engage, and how we love.

There's no right or wrong way to raise kids, it will always look different for everyone. But to the limit we allow the love of God to fill our mind, body, and spirit, will drastically have an impact on how we show the love of God to our children. For us to fully love in a whole and prospering way, we must first know the love of God for ourselves. From the depths of our knowing, we are able to give, to influence, and to raise up our own kids.

Let's go back to the beginning. God is love. Love isn't a word that only describes the character of God, but God is the originator of what love is. The character and nature of God is something that cannot change. God cannot deny who He is, and nothing He does comes from a selfish or evil place. God is love, it is who He is and who He always will be. Therefore, friend, you are so loved! There is nothing you can do about that. It's not your choice, it's just a fact that simply will never change because God Himself is unchanging. A part of your core identity flows the truth that you are deeply loved. The reason you were created was from the overflowing of love and unity within the Trinity. Being loved by the eternal God is not dependent on how well you do life or what you achieve this side of heaven - it is purely because your creator loves you, and nothing can separate you from that.

This is what the Lord says in Isaiah 54:10. It hits the sweet spot of my heart every time I read it. **"For the mountains may depart and the hills be removed, but my steadfast love shall not depart from you, and my covenant of peace shall not be removed, "says the Lord, who has compassion on you."**

Essentially what I hear God saying in this passage is that everything else in life can come and go, all will pass away, but His love is permanent. When there was nothing, there was God's love, and whatever comes, there is God's love. We can rest in that assurance.

SO WE HAVE COME TO KNOW AND TO BELIEVE THE LOVE THAT
GOD HAS FOR US. GOD IS LOVE, AND WHOEVER ABIDES
IN LOVE ABIDES IN GOD, AND GOD ABIDES IN HIM.
- 1 JOHN 4:16 ESV -

BELOVED, LET US LOVE ONE ANOTHER, FOR LOVE IS FROM GOD,
AND WHOEVER LOVES HAS BEEN BORN OF GOD AND KNOWS GOD.
- 1 JOHN 4:7 ESV -

FOR I AM SURE THAT NEITHER DEATH NOR LIFE, NOR ANGELS,
NOR RULERS, NOR THINGS PRESENT, NOR THINGS TO COME,
NOR POWERS, NOR HEIGHT, NOR DEPTH, NOR ANYTHING ELSE
IN ALL CREATION, WILL BE ABLE TO SEPARATE US FROM THE
LOVE OF GOD IN CHRIST JESUS OUR LORD.
- ROMANS 8:38-39 ESV -

"FOR THE MOUNTAINS MAY DEPART AND THE HILLS BE REMOVED,
BUT MY STEADFAST LOVE SHALL NOT DEPART FROM YOU, AND MY
COVENANT OF PEACE SHALL NOT BE REMOVED," SAYS THE LORD,
WHO HAS COMPASSION ON YOU.
- ISAIAH 54:10 ESV -

AS THE FATHER HAS LOVED ME, SO HAVE I LOVED YOU.
ABIDE IN MY LOVE.
- JOHN 15:9 ESV -

In your own words, what does it mean to abide in God's love?

Take a few moments now and listen to God. Ask Him to speak to you about His love for you. Write down what He says below.

Knowing that you are loved by God, how does that influence you as a mom?

P r a y e r : Father, it is only through Your love that I am fully myself and fully alive. This world brings darkness and hardships, but I ask that You would begin to take me back to Your love. Let it break through the walls I have built within myself, let it transform my mind and how I live. Thank You for being love. Thank You that You sent Jesus to make all things new. Help me to understand that I am loved by You, and that through Your love I can love others in the best and sincerest way.

- Amen

Check out the Trek Further section at the end of this book to apply today's lesson to your real life.

12

I AM MAMA HEAR ME ROAR

Has someone ever said this to you ... "Oh, it must be so nice not working. I wish I could do what you do. What a nice break being home with the kids." You guys, too many times. I won't expand too much on this, but I want to say if that's happened to you, just shrug it off. Sometimes people are naive, and a lot of time people tend to have a "life is always greener on the other side" mentality. If they don't understand, it's okay. Just breathe in, breathe out, let it go ... bless them. (Preaching to myself.)

I want to tell you a lie. Tell me if this sounds familiar.

You are weak and meek. You are a woman, and a mother, therefore your place is only in the home raising kids and doing housework. The men do the real hard stuff, you just need to be supportive of his calling and learn to cook well and fold fitted sheets.

Don't dream big, what's the point? All you do is change diapers and pick up messes. You're basically disappearing as a person. You're not a force to be reckoned with. How can you really make a difference for God's kingdom when you can't even get your little to-do list done? Just stay home, stay quiet, stay busy.

I have heard statements like the ones above voiced by my peers and also in my own thought life. We have accepted so many lies of the enemy on what motherhood is all about. "Keep quiet. Stay home. Ministry is for other people. You can't influence. You aren't seen." The enemy wants nothing more than for you to believe that your role as a mom and as a wife is second best. He will use every bad day, every hormonal change, every difficult situation to shut you down. He does this because He knows that women, that mothers, that wives, carry aspects of God's character, and an assignment from heaven that is absolutely world changing.

It was through Eve that God revealed His glory to mankind. It was through Mary that God brought forth the Savior of the world. It was through Esther that a nation was saved. It didn't have to be that way, but He chose it to be that way. Maybe even as a reminder to us that we have a role to play. It was through countless women who knew their identity in God that He moved in powerful ways throughout history.

Nothing has changed today. You have been given an assignment by God to raise and disciple the next generation. You have also been given assignments from God to fulfill other dreams and ministry callings. We tend to think motherhood is our "hidden season." But I believe motherhood is a powerful season of ministry. Nothing is truly hidden. How we raise our kids, how we love our neighbors, how we love Jesus, or how we don't, will be seen and accounted for. Ministry, loving God and others fully, isn't for later, it's for now. Don't believe the lie that says "one day" or "when I'm done raising kids I'll impact others." You guys, the way you love your family will impact others. The way you live your life now is a testament to others.

If God is calling you to put some dreams and desires on the shelf for now, and be fully present at home, then you make those lunches, and read those bedtime stories like a boss. Whatever assignment He has called you into now, and in the future, you can walk it out with power and authority.

How we show Jesus to others will look different in different seasons of our lives. But in every season, whether we are aware of it or not, we will be sharing a story to those around us. What gospel are we telling?

Loving Jesus means that we have all been called to make disciples. All, called. He didn't say "Well except you moms because you aren't really capable of much more than housework and making babies. This is just a call for the men." No! There are little disciples running around your house right now. Start there. Don't miss the depth of importance your role as a mother is in expanding God's kingdom and making disciples that make disciples. And it doesn't stop there God will expand your reach of influence. If you allow His Holy Spirit to actively guide you in your life He will highlight friends that need coffee dates He will give you something encouraging to say to the lady at the cash register, He will place people on your heart to intercede for. Maybe He will lead you to start a ministry, begin a Bible study, take a certain career path, or who knows?

You are a force in the kingdom of God, because you have been created and called by God.

Remember, it's not about what we do, it's about loving God and walking in obedience to the things He calls us to. Ministry looks like a life lived for Christ, loving God, loving others, walking in obedience with His Spirit.

Let's wrap up today with a strong truth...

A mom stands strong on the truth of God's word. She knows her identity is within Christ, and she approaches the gift of motherhood as a heavenly assignment of discipleship. She is a leader, an influencer, a comforter and a strong force against the enemy. Her assignment is far from low key and second best. She is a world changer, an image bearer, a bright light in the darkness, strong and courageous in all things.

Now Say it with me...I am mama, hear me roar!

THE SPIRIT OF THE LORD GOD IS UPON ME, BECAUSE THE LORD HAS ANOINTED ME TO BRING GOOD NEWS TO THE POOR; HE HAS SENT ME TO BIND UP THE BROKENHEARTED, TO PROCLAIM LIBERTY TO THE CAPTIVES, AND THE OPENING OF THE PRISON TO THOSE WHO ARE BOUND; TO PROCLAIM THE YEAR OF THE LORD'S FAVOR, AND THE DAY OF VENGEANCE OF OUR GOD; TO COMFORT ALL WHO MOURN; TO GRANT TO THOSE WHO MOURN IN ZION—TO GIVE THEM A BEAUTIFUL HEADDRESS INSTEAD OF ASHES, THE OIL OF GLADNESS INSTEAD OF MOURNING, THE GARMENT OF PRAISE INSTEAD OF A FAINT SPIRIT; THAT THEY MAY BE CALLED OAKS OF RIGHTEOUSNESS, THE PLANTING OF THE LORD, THAT HE MAY BE GLORIFIED. THEY SHALL BUILD UP THE ANCIENT RUINS; THEY SHALL RAISE UP THE FORMER DEVASTATIONS; THEY SHALL REPAIR THE RUINED CITIES, THE DEVASTATIONS OF MANY GENERATIONS. STRANGERS SHALL STAND AND TEND YOUR FLOCKS; FOREIGNERS SHALL BE YOUR PLOWMEN AND VINEDRESSERS; BUT YOU SHALL BE CALLED THE PRIESTS OF THE LORD; THEY SHALL SPEAK OF YOU AS THE MINISTERS OF OUR GOD; YOU SHALL EAT THE WEALTH OF THE NATIONS, AND IN THEIR GLORY YOU SHALL BOAST. INSTEAD OF YOUR SHAME THERE SHALL BE A DOUBLE PORTION; INSTEAD OF DISHONOR THEY SHALL REJOICE IN THEIR LOT; THEREFORE IN THEIR LAND THEY SHALL POSSESS A DOUBLE PORTION; THEY SHALL HAVE EVERLASTING JOY. FOR I THE LORD LOVE JUSTICE; I HATE ROBBERY AND WRONG; I WILL FAITHFULLY GIVE THEM THEIR RECOMPENSE, AND I WILL MAKE AN EVERLASTING COVENANT WITH THEM. THEIR OFFSPRING SHALL BE KNOWN AMONG THE NATIONS, AND THEIR DESCENDANTS IN THE MIDST OF THE PEOPLES; ALL WHO SEE THEM SHALL ACKNOWLEDGE THEM, THAT THEY ARE AN OFFSPRING THE LORD HAS BLESSED. I WILL GREATLY REJOICE IN THE LORD; MY SOUL SHALL EXULT IN MY GOD, FOR HE HAS CLOTHED ME WITH THE GARMENTS OF SALVATION; HE HAS COVERED ME WITH THE ROBE OF RIGHTEOUSNESS, AS A BRIDEGROOM DECKS HIMSELF LIKE A PRIEST WITH A BEAUTIFUL HEADDRESS, AND AS A BRIDE ADORNS HERSELF WITH HER JEWELS. FOR AS THE EARTH BRINGS FORTH ITS SPROUTS, AND AS A GARDEN CAUSES WHAT IS SOWN IN IT TO SPROUT UP, SO THE LORD GOD WILL CAUSE RIGHTEOUSNESS AND PRAISE TO SPROUT UP BEFORE ALL THE NATIONS.
- ISAIAH 61 ESV -

What lies have you heard about motherhood? Have you ever felt like being a mom is second best? Write down a time you had this experience.

In your own words, journal what God is speaking to you personally through today's devotional.

Isaiah 61 proclaims part of our destiny as people who are in relationship with God. Reading this passage, what verses awaken deeper parts of your heart?

Prayer : Thank You for making women and men. Thank You that through both genders Your character and nature is made known to us. Thank You for calling women, moms, and wives to dream big and do great things for Your kingdom. We know that through Your grace, and through the Holy Spirit, we can be world changers. Thank You for calling me into this role as a mom. I ask that You will help me see this role as a heavenly assignment, a gift, and an important journey. I love You so much.

- Amen

Check out the Trek Further section at the end of this book to apply today's lesson to your real life.

You are seen, deeply loved, full of grace, and you can do hard things because God is made perfect in your weakness. He has equipped you through grace and through the power of His Spirit to climb every mountain and walk through every valley.

TOOLS FOR MOTHERHOOD

week three

13

THE MAGIC WORD

We ask our kids to say the magic word when they want something. "Please!" As moms, more times than not, the magic word we need to learn is "no." No to things that take time, energy, and effort away from the things that truly matter.

We have arrived at adulthood, ya'll. To the land of responsibility, decision making, and living out our destiny. These are the best of times and the hardest of times. Let's just all get on the same page for a second. Not to be a Debbie downer, but it's important to know that we can't be it all, do it all, and succeed at everything. To live this life well, we must learn what our priorities are, and start saying no to more, so we can say yes to what is important.

This journey of motherhood will undoubtedly confront you with life's greatest balancing act. After I had my first child it was hard for me to fully surrender to the new change of pace. I wanted to be involved with ministry like I had been in the past. I was trying to continue life as it always had been and, on top of that, be a fulltime mom. It wasn't long until I realized that it was simply not possible to have both fully. Something had to give. I needed to hone in on what God was asking me to steward in that season, and put some things on the shelf for later.

What I found was that being busy, productive, a to-do list master, a ninja-at-all-things-life kind of mother, wasn't the best life out there for me. A simpler, less busy, less crowded, more intentional life was best. The struggle is that what is modeled around us usually gravitates to the packed agenda, "on" the go, mama style. That lifestyle says, more equals purposeful. More says, "look what I can do, I've got this ship under control."

But really, more equals exhausted. And every "yes" is a "no" to something else. Life is more about being firmly planted in Christ and fully present in each moment that God has given us. It's about offering our best selves to the people in front of us, not the leftovers. In the end, we will see that what matters most are the relationships we have cultivated and the legacy we leave behind. Whether we choose to love Jesus with all of our being and love our neighbours as an overflow of that love, will either be our greatest regret or our greatest accomplishment.

The enemy would like nothing more than to make you believe that being busy (even with ministry) equals serving God well. Busyness, in any area of life, can be our greatest distraction from God.

Motherhood involves being thoughtful, prayerful, and intentional about our time and activities. We were never meant to live a chaotic life. Sure, we have our days, but when we ask God what He has specifically for us in this season, we can start walking more intentionally on the path He has set for us. Hear me on this. This is not an invitation to laziness. This is not a justification for you to never serve and never invest. This is about using wisdom in what God is asking you to say yes and no to right now.

Setting boundaries for you and your family might bother people. Saying no to volunteering or helping with this thing or that, might make some people upset. That's okay. Part of saying yes and no involves being okay with not pleasing everyone. This might be the biggest hurdle to overcome, but it doesn't outweigh the importance of a healthy and holistic lifestyle. Our value isn't in who we are to others, or what we can do for people, the church, or our jobs. Jesus holds all value and worthiness in His hands for us. While God is limitless in His capacity to do anything, we were created with limitations, physically and emotionally. Let's be intentional about who we are investing in, who we hang out with, and in what we involve ourselves. Ask God, what do You have for me in this season, right now?

If we look at the way Jesus lived, we can see that He was an expert at knowing where to put His efforts and where to not. He loved everyone, but He invested in His disciples, training them to go and invest in others. He took time to be with the Father instead of over working and burning out. This is our goal as well: Be intentional in how we use the time, energy, and giftings that we have.

"AWAKE, O SLEEPER, AND ARISE FROM THE DEAD, AND CHRIST
WILL SHINE ON YOU." LOOK CAREFULLY THEN HOW YOU WALK, NOT
AS UNWISE BUT AS WISE, MAKING THE BEST USE OF THE TIME,
BECAUSE THE DAYS ARE EVIL. THEREFORE, DO NOT BE FOOLISH, BUT
UNDERSTAND WHAT THE WILL OF THE LORD IS. AND DO NOT GET DRUNK
WITH WINE, FOR THAT IS DEBAUCHERY, BUT BE FILLED WITH THE SPIRIT,
ADDRESSING ONE ANOTHER IN PSALMS AND HYMNS AND SPIRITUAL
SONGS, SINGING AND MAKING MELODY TO THE LORD WITH YOUR
HEART, GIVING THANKS ALWAYS AND FOR EVERYTHING TO GOD THE
FATHER IN THE NAME OF OUR LORD JESUS CHRIST, SUBMITTING TO ONE
ANOTHER OUT OF REVERENCE FOR CHRIST.
- EPHESIANS 5:14-21 ESV -

LOOK CAREFULLY THEN HOW YOU WALK, NOT AS UNWISE BUT
AS WISE, MAKING THE BEST USE OF THE TIME, BECAUSE THE DAYS
ARE EVIL. THEREFORE, DO NOT BE FOOLISH, BUT UNDERSTAND
WHAT THE WILL OF THE LORD IS.
- EPHESIANS 5:15-17 ESV -

What distracts you from being fully present?

In what ways have you found fulfillment and comfort in being busy?

Is God highlighting an area of your life that you need to slow down in or even stop completely?

Prayer : Father, thank You for not being a God who loves us for what we are capable of doing. Thank You for giving us people and certain assignments to invest in and accomplish for Your glory. I pray that You would help me to reevaluate my life today. Help me see where I'm striving for other people's approval or an area of my heart that believes I am worthless unless I'm always working. Help me to set healthy, God-given boundaries in my life so that I can do what You have asked me to do well. I love You.

- Amen

Check out the Trek Further section at the end of this book to apply today's lesson to your real life.

14

LEGACY

Legacy. When I joined Josh's family I gained the privilege of meeting some of Josh's extended family, seven siblings known as "the Frenches." They are well into the second half of their lives, serving and loving Jesus wholeheartedly. Seven, hard-of-hearing, slow-walking, God-fearing siblings have taught me a lot about legacy. They speak often of the important things in life, the things that last far after we are gone. They are intentional in their prayer life, sharing stories of God's faithfulness, and centering all things around bringing Jesus glory. It's like muscle memory to them, like breathing and sleeping. Jesus all day, in all things.

I always leave encouraged after a weekend with the Frenches. They inspire me to get serious about my relationship with Jesus and to go after Him more fiercely. Recently I have been inspired to get serious about the legacy I leave my family and the generations to come. Ya'll, it starts now. It starts as we build our homes and form traditions with our families, as we respond to crises and victories, and as we choose how to love our kids. One day when they leave the threshold of our home, what will they carry with them? What will they have in their metaphorical backpacks of life? What values, habits, truths, perspectives? What will they multiply as they start their own families?

Does this overwhelm you to think about? I'm raising my hand high over here because it does to me. We are all doing our best, right? Days when I'm just done and my kids are on their fourth rerun of Frozen, I kind of feel like I'm failing. Sometimes I feel like I don't have time to think about the legacy I'm building. It's easy to feel like this is

unnecessary to dwell on now, but folks, that's a lie. These are things we should be thinking about. The legacy we leave within our home is extremely important. Another reason why being a mom isn't a "no big deal thing." We set a tone and a pattern that our little ones see. We, as parents, hold the sole responsibility to bring our children up in the Lord. *Us*, not the pastor or the teacher or the family friends.

Josh's grandmother, Helen, who is one of the seven French siblings, prays for all of her children and their children every day. Every day. No one sees this. This is done in the quiet and secret of her home. No one may know about her diligent prayer life, but those she prays for have reaped the blessing of her prayers. That act of obedience has impacted me and my prayer life in so many ways.

Let me say it again: we will never fulfill every spiritual and emotional need of our kids. The Father can do that, not us. But we introduce our kids to the Father, and we set an example of the kingdom within our home. We will always be learning and growing, and messing up and trying again. It's about doing what we can, sometimes big, but most times small, that can create a home environment where our children can experience Jesus.

Here are a few gems I have learned from legacy builders - storytelling, prayer, and interior decorating. The Bible speaks often of storytelling.God intended that parents pass on stories of God's faithfulness from generation to generation. The stories in the Bible, and our own personal testimonies, are meant to be shared with our kids. Sharing the Word of God, even from infancy, will build a spirit that is sensitive to hearing God's voice. There is no such thing as a "little" Holy Spirit, and our kids carry the same presence of God that we do. Their souls are thirsty and ready to hear and know the Word of God. We are storytellers, people who share of God's goodness, sing songs of His love, and spiritually nurture the souls of our kids with the good news of Jesus.

Secondly, prayer. God doesn't ask for long, dragged out prayers. In fact, He wants us to get to the point already. Small, but powerful prayers for our children as we wash dishes, drop them off at school, or as we tuck them into bed, will create an atmosphere of intercession and blessing within our home. It isn't seen, but it is felt. Josh and I have prayed Numbers 6:24-26 over each of our children every night before they sleep. My three-year-old daughter now can almost recite the whole blessing on her own. We started this because Josh's parents did the same for him when we was growing up. And because we are creatures of habit, Josh did the same in our family. What is done in the home diligently, will be passed down, the good and the bad.

Lastly, let's not forget about the home. I'm obsessed with "DIY." If I wasn't careful, all my money would go to yarn, glue, and fabrics ... lots and lots of fabrics. I was challenged once with the question "Does your home tell the story of the gospel?" My first reaction was "Uh...Does it have to?" I thought about this for awhile and finally understood what the question was really asking. When people come into my home, would they question my love for God? What lingering feeling or impression do they take away? Is my home a place that provides peace, rest, and a tangible representation of the

Holy Spirit, or does it tell a different story? I believe there are two things to look at here. One is focused on the physical impression. If you were to come to my house you would notice a variety of genres of books on the shelves, you would either hear Bethel worship or Justin Timberlake playing on our Spotify, and most likely a funny quote about tacos would be on my letterboard on my kitchen wall. It's not about throwing out everything that isn't strictly about God, but it is about purging things that offend God. We aren't part of a religion; we are in a relationship with God. You wouldn't have a photo of your ex-boyfriend framed on the wall next to your wedding photos would you?

Let's not forget about the atmosphere in the home. I'm a sucker for a good coffee shop, and let's be honest, if it's atmosphere is off, guaranteed the coffee won't taste good. We can't see feelings, but we do experience them, and that also goes for our home. If we are living a life that produces anger, pride, and other sinful fruit, then that's the feeling people will experience when they are in our home. Practicing a life that produces the fruit of the Spirit at home will be the take away that our kids and guests feel when they leave. Making the home a place of peace, safety and comfort will be a ministry to your family but also to everyone who is invited in.

I can't tell you how many times I have tried to start a new thing in our home, like eating dinners together, or having family devotionals, and it is just a pure disaster. When that happens, my husband and I go back to God and ask for new ideas. Every family is different, and there is no "right" way to be a family. Try things that are true to what your family loves to do and what works in your life. No one will do it perfectly, and no one will have it all together. It's about being mindful of the legacy we are leaving and being obedient to God's calling as parents to raise our kids to know who He is. Starting somewhere is the first and best step.

TRAIN UP A CHILD IN THE WAY HE SHOULD GO;
EVEN WHEN HE IS OLD HE WILL NOT DEPART FROM IT.
- PROVERBS 22:6 ESV -

ONE GENERATION SHALL COMMEND YOUR WORKS
TO ANOTHER, AND SHALL DECLARE YOUR MIGHTY ACTS.
- PSALM 145:4 ESV -

GIVE EAR, O MY PEOPLE, TO MY TEACHING; INCLINE YOUR EARS TO THE WORDS OF
MY MOUTH! I WILL OPEN MY MOUTH IN A PARABLE; I WILL UTTER DARK SAYINGS
FROM OF OLD, THINGS THAT WE HAVE HEARD AND KNOWN, THAT OUR FATHERS HAVE
TOLD US. WE WILL NOT HIDE THEM FROM THEIR CHILDREN, BUT TELL TO THE COMING
GENERATION THE GLORIOUS DEEDS OF THE LORD, AND HIS MIGHT, AND THE WONDERS
THAT HE HAS DONE. HE ESTABLISHED A TESTIMONY IN JACOB AND APPOINTED A LAW
IN ISRAEL, WHICH HE COMMANDED OUR FATHERS TO TEACH TO THEIR CHILDREN, THAT
THE NEXT GENERATION MIGHT KNOW THEM, THE CHILDREN YET UNBORN, AND ARISE
AND TELL THEM TO THEIR CHILDREN, SO THAT THEY SHOULD SET THEIR HOPE IN GOD
AND NOT FORGET THE WORKS OF GOD, BUT KEEP HIS COMMANDMENTS; AND
THAT THEY SHOULD NOT BE LIKE THEIR FATHERS, A STUBBORN AND REBELLIOUS
GENERATION, A GENERATION WHOSE HEART WAS NOT STEADFAST, WHOSE SPIRIT
WAS NOT FAITHFUL TO GOD.
- PSALM 78:1-8 ESV -

THE LIVING, THE LIVING, HE THANKS YOU, AS I DO THIS DAY;
THE FATHER MAKES KNOWN TO THE CHILDREN YOUR FAITHFULNESS.
- ISAIAH 38:19 ESV -

NUMBERS 6:24-26 IS THE BLESSING JOSH AND I HAVE PRAYED OVER OUR TWO
GIRLS EVERY NIGHT. MAKING THIS PRAYER A RHYTHM IN OUR EVERYDAY IS ONE WAY
WE ARE INTENTIONALLY PASSING ON GOD'S WORD AND PRAYER TO OUR KIDS.
IT'S A SIMPLE HABIT THAT HAS A LASTING LEGACY.

THE LORD BLESS YOU AND KEEP YOU; THE LORD MAKE HIS FACE TO
SHINE UPON YOU AND BE GRACIOUS TO YOU; THE LORD LIFT UP HIS
COUNTENANCE UPON YOU AND GIVE YOU PEACE.
- NUMBERS 6:24-26 ESV -

What was the legacy your parents passed on to you?

_____

_____

_____

_____

_____

What are a few things you want to begin doing to leave a better legacy for your children?

_____

_____

_____

_____

What is God speaking to you through this message?

_____

_____

_____

_____

_____

Prayer : Father, we acknowledge that Jesus left the greatest legacy of all for us. He perfectly showed us how to live a full life loving and living for You. Despite the family we have come from and the things we have experienced, would You help us to make the changes we need to in our personal life to rightly influence the coming generations. Show us where we can leave a legacy of Your faithfulness, in prayer, and even in our own homes. Thank You for inviting us into Your story, and for the privilege it is to love and honor You.

- Amen

Check out the Trek Further section at the end of this book to apply today's lesson to your real life.

15

LOVE YOURSELF

We may rock at changing diapers and multitasking, but let's face it, we can be pretty bad at taking care of ourselves.

"Today, I give you permission to love yourself." The first time a friend of mine said that to me, I literally laughed in her face. *With what time? And isn't that selfish?* But she was right, it's so important, and we miss the value of this discipline too often as moms. In the gospels, we discover the second of the greatest commandments from God, "Love your neighbor as yourself." Matthew 22:39 ESV We take to heart the "love your neighbor" part, and then we just kind of skim over the "as yourself" line.

The truth is we can only give what we have. If we are not valuing our own physical and spiritual health, then we will be giving our family the leftovers instead of our best selves. Self-care isn't a selfish act; it isn't a bonus that we get if we have time. It's important and worth prioritizing. The journey of figuring out what loving myself looks like in the middle of somewhat crazy days has been, well, pretty much impossible. It's challenging and often differs day to day. And that's okay. We are in the stage of "rolling with the punches," of "winging it" and doing the best we can, hoping we can mark some things off the to-do list. There is grace, and self-care isn't going to look the same for everyone. But I believe it's important to the heart of God. I believe He threw in the "as yourself" line as a twofold reminder. One, because He cares deeply about you and wants you to live a beautiful life in your true identity as His. And secondly, because He knows that when we love who we are in Him, and take time to maintain a healthy lifestyle for ourselves, we can even more deeply love those around us.

We are all humans with capacities, humans that need to be poured into and filled with a growing relationship with God. Maybe this looks like sipping a hot drink at your favorite café, going for a walk, or joining a book club or Bible study group. Sometimes it's as simple as having a night-time routine that allows you to slow down and pamper a bit. It probably won't always be as much as you would like, and it might not feel like it's enough, but start somewhere. Keep your expectations realistic and pay attention to the little things that feed your soul, creating time to focus inward.

Loving yourself and self-worship are very different. Jesus calls us to love others as we love ourselves in Christ, not to raise ourselves up in a place of idolizing or pride. It's through our identity in Christ, being created by Him for relationship with Him, that we can love who we are because He loves us. When we see ourselves as part of the bride of Christ, His Church, then we no longer hate who we are, but we love who God has created us to be.

FOR NO ONE EVER HATED HIS OWN FLESH, BUT NOURISHES AND CHERISHES IT, JUST AS CHRIST DOES THE CHURCH, BECAUSE WE ARE MEMBERS OF HIS BODY.
- EPHESIANS 5:29-30 ESV -

AND HE SAID TO HIM, YOU SHALL LOVE THE LORD YOUR GOD WITH ALL YOUR HEART AND WITH ALL YOUR SOUL AND WITH ALL YOUR MIND. THIS IS THE GREAT AND FIRST COMMANDMENT. AND A SECOND IS LIKE IT: YOU SHALL LOVE YOUR NEIGHBOR AS YOURSELF.
- MATTHEW 22:37-39 ESV -

What activities bring you joy and refreshment?

What are you currently doing to take care of your mind, body, and spirit?

What holds you back from investing in self-care?

What is God speaking to you through this message?

Prayer : Father, thank You for caring about my emotional, physical, and spiritual health. Thank You for speaking to me about the importance of taking care of the body and soul You have given me so I can in turn love and care for others. Help me decipher the difference between selfishness and loving myself because of my identity in You. Ultimately, help me to be a woman who overflows with love and care for others, allowing others to experience the love of Jesus within me.

- Amen

Check out the Trek Further section at the end of this book to apply today's lesson to your real life.

16

LOVE
YOUR
MAN

Let's be real. Kids just change things. They are blessings, and they bring so much joy, but our relationships, schedules, and way of life take a huge shift when these little humans arrive. This journey of parenthood on which we have embarked on, God has given us the gift of a partner, a husband. Parenthood is meant to be done together.

Why marriage? Because love beckons covenant. Like our creator, we desire unconditional love.

The greatest love of all was given to us through Jesus Christ. He embodied the fullness of God's character and nature, which is love. The Father loved us so much, that He gave, that He died, for us. When we come to know Jesus, our heart wants to do the same in return, to give, and to die to our own desires in pursuit of His will. Marriage is a visual representation of that giving and dying that Christ did for us, to the world. We enter into covenant with someone as Christ did with us, and we vow that through better or worse, sickness and

in health, for richer or poorer, we are all in, giving ourselves, dying to ourselves, loving the other above ourselves. Agape love blows the world's standard of love out of the water. Marriage with Jesus at the center and as the foundation can mirror to the world a love worth knowing and wanting.

If you've been married for more than five minutes, you will know that you have married a real-life human being. Not a perfect person that reads your mind and anticipates all your needs. A person who just like you, has faults, strengths and weaknesses, and good and bad qualities. I believe marriage is one of God's greatest gifts to us and a beautiful, real-life model of the Father's love towards us. That is also why I believe Satan puts so much effort into the destruction of marriage. If he can succeed in destroying and distorting the kingdom purpose of marriage, it will misrepresent an aspect of God to the world.

When we picture motherhood as a trail that we

are embarking on, we are not walking that path alone. The partnership of marriage and in parenting is rich and beautiful, and made for extraordinary purpose. It's not the easy, lovey-dovey things that make it rich, it's the hard choices and compromise and sacrifice that give it depth and fullness.

Marriage can be hard. Some of you are now thinking, "well that's the understatement of the year!" But it's true, marriage takes work, intentionality, dying to yourself, preferring the other above yourself, and giving yourself fully to another. Sounds a lot like looking more and more like Jesus, huh?

In motherhood, marriage will get hard. When the pressure comes, when life feels unbalanced, when you feel like you're losing a bit of your former self, that is when the enemy will want tension and strife to enter into your marriage. The arguments and the accusations that can come up when you lack sleep and have poor eating habits are incredible. Raising kids can be a perfect storm for conflict, if you allow it. But, if our minds are focused heavenward, and we know and recognize the gift and purpose of marriage, we will approach it differently than the world.

I remember having a very honest and transparent conversation with a group of friends once about marriage. One by one, confessions started to be made. With each confession it was like the shame in the room lifted as each woman said, "I can relate. I thought I was the only one." Things like, "I use to want to have sex and now I dread it", or, "sometimes I find other men attractive and not my own husband", and, "I feel unappreciated and totally misunderstood from my husband", "I feel like we don't know each other anymore". The confessions flowed out, and relief set in as each woman realized they weren't alone.

The fact is that real love is a choice, not a feeling. This is agape love. In the Greek language, the word "agape" refers to unconditional love. Love that isn't dependent on circumstances or what it can gain. Agape love is the love of God towards us. Agape love is different than sexual desire. It isn't transactional, where you give only because you get something in return. In the New Testament when Jesus speaks of loving one another, and when He speaks of the love of God, He is using the Greek word, agape.

We are called to agape love our husbands. Agape love chooses to love, not depending on our emotions and feelings. Through the picture of marriage we show the world a different kind of love. We show them the Father's love, agape love. Even in our weakness, even in our sin, even when things are hard, He chooses to love us unconditionally. The world says that if you are unhappy you should leave him. The world says, "think only about yourself and don't let anyone get in your way." The world says, "love is a feeling, and if the feelings leave then you have the right to as well." God's story of love is different and should be represented differently within marriage. When it's hard, you stay and work it out. When the other is suffering, you suffer with them. When you are unhappy with your husband, you find your joy in Jesus and ask the question, "how can I love him like God loves me?" When the feelings aren't there like they use to be, you choose to walk in a love that is much deeper than chemical reactions. Marriage with Christ as the center and with the intention of the kingdom of God tell a very different story to the world.

So today, if you're in the trenches in your marriage I want you to know that you're not the only one, I also want you to know that you have a choice to make. We have the choice to love with the agape love of Christ, love only when it benefits us, or when we feel like it. Loving God means seeking His kingdom first and loving your husband with the agape love.

IN THIS THE LOVE OF GOD WAS MADE MANIFEST AMONG US, THAT GOD SENT HIS ONLY SON INTO THE WORLD, SO THAT WE MIGHT LIVE THROUGH HIM. IN THIS IS LOVE, NOT THAT WE HAVE LOVED GOD BUT THAT HE LOVED US AND SENT HIS SON TO BE THE PROPITIATION FOR OUR SINS. BELOVED, IF GOD SO LOVED US, WE ALSO OUGHT TO LOVE ONE ANOTHER. NO ONE HAS EVER SEEN GOD; IF WE LOVE ONE ANOTHER, GOD ABIDES IN US AND HIS LOVE IS PERFECTED IN US.
- 1 JOHN 4:9-12 ESV -

THIS IS MY COMMANDMENT, THAT YOU LOVE ONE ANOTHER AS I HAVE LOVED YOU. GREATER LOVE HAS NO ONE THAN THIS, THAT SOMEONE LAY DOWN HIS LIFE FOR HIS FRIENDS.
- JOHN 15:12-13 ESV -

In your own words, how does marriage reflect God's nature?

How is your relationship with your husband right now? In what areas are you doing well? Where are you struggling?

How can you better extend agape love to your husband?
Is God highlighting a specific part of your relationship?

Prayer : Father, thank You for being the perfect example of true love. Thank You for giving all of yourself for me so that I can be fully alive in You. Thank You for showing me what it looks like to love my husband with the kind of love that You have towards us. I ask that You would help me to see my husband through Your eyes, and help show me how I can love him more. I pray for my marriage to be a true representation of kingdom love to the people I know and to the world. Holy Spirit help me to glorify You in my marriage.

- Amen

Check out the Trek Further section at the end of this book to apply today's lesson to your real life.

17 SISTERHOOD IN MOTHERHOOD

We all need a tribe. In fact, God intended for all of us to live with a tribal mentality. We've heard the saying, "it takes a village" when it comes to raising kids, but I also believe it takes a sisterhood to be in motherhood. There is something deep within each of us that desires relationship, and that desire stems from the nature of God within the Trinity. At the core of our design we were meant to live, grow, and walk, alongside other people. It was never God's intention for us to walk through life alone. Just as the Father, Jesus, and Holy Spirit are in perfect unity, in complete oneness, we, being created in God's likeness, are made for the same unity with each other. Motherhood isn't meant to be journeyed and lived alone. Not only do we need each other, but we become more like Jesus when we choose to enter into relationships with others.

Being part of a tribe, a sisterhood, means that we expose our weaknesses and strengths to others. The fear of being truly known, of vulnerability, of exposing that you actually *need* help, is a scary thing. We all want to be super mom, running errands, raising kids, loving our husbands, and still giving the impression it all comes naturally. But here's the thing, Jesus, the Son of God, needed friends. He spent His days sharing meals, ministering, traveling, and just hanging out with the guys we know as the 12 disciples. Jesus chose to invest and be known by this group of men. He showed us how important it is to be part of a tribe.

Relationships are messy. Investing in people and being vulnerable will for sure have moments of pain and disappointment, at least if you're doing it right. This is also part of the beauty of relationship. We learn and grow so much when we choose to link arms with others and become more like Christ. Like iron sharpens iron, you need sisters who point you to Jesus, who are committed to seeing the kingdom of God manifest in your life, who bring over soup when the stomach flu hits your home, binge watch Gilmore Girls, and stand with you in joys and in sufferings. Sisterhood is a powerful, purposeful gift from God.

Maybe this is easier said than done.

We live in a culture like none before, where so much of our lives can be viewed and shared through social media platforms. I'm not saying social media is bad, but I am saying that if we aren't careful, before we know it, feelings of comparison, jealousy, and envy can rise up between us and other women. We were meant to be a sisterhood, to be a gender that

represents aspects of God's glory, and who love each other with the love of Christ within us. We were never meant to walk against each other but rather beside one another, spurring each other on towards God.

The enemy has succeeded in so many ways to pin women against other women. He has successfully convinced many women to view other women as the competition. He has tempted us to separate into groups against one another based on the color of our skin, the way we raise our kids, and even by the clothes we wear. He wants us to measure our own value and success based on what we see other moms doing on instagram and blogs. Sounds like elementary school drama, but we still do it as adults. As a result, women have missed out on the fullness of the calling God has given them because they are too focused on how they don't measure up and what other women are accomplishing. We have missed out on deep, fulfilling, purposeful relationships with one another.

As Christian women, we have a responsibility to represent Jesus to others. We look at life with kingdom perspective. We turn from selfishness and sin, and run towards love and holiness. And it's possible because Jesus is within us. What I'm saying is, walk against, no, run against the flow of comparison and tearing down other women. Be a woman who embraces a tribe of her own, and encourages, empowers, and lifts up other women, even the ones who are "prettier" and "smarter" than you. When you live this way, you allow yourself to live a freer, more joyful, less stressful, more fulfilling life.

You were created by relationship, for relationship. When the world says, "compete with others" and "you don't need anyone", go against that flow and reach out, form a sisterhood.

BEHOLD, HOW GOOD AND PLEASANT IT IS
WHEN BROTHERS DWELL IN UNITY!
- PSALM 133:1 ESV -

A TRANQUIL HEART GIVES LIFE TO THE FLESH,
BUT ENVY MAKES THE BONES ROT.
- PROVERBS 14:30 ESV -

BY THIS ALL PEOPLE WILL KNOW THAT YOU ARE
MY DISCIPLES, IF YOU HAVE LOVE FOR ONE ANOTHER.
- JOHN 13:35 ESV -

PUT ON THEN, AS GOD'S CHOSEN ONES, HOLY AND BELOVED,
COMPASSIONATE HEARTS, KINDNESS, HUMILITY, MEEKNESS,
AND PATIENCE, BEARING WITH ONE ANOTHER AND, IF ONE HAS
A COMPLAINT AGAINST ANOTHER, FORGIVING EACH OTHER;
AS THE LORD HAS FORGIVEN YOU, SO YOU ALSO MUST FORGIVE.
AND ABOVE ALL THESE PUT ON LOVE, WHICH BINDS EVERYTHING
TOGETHER IN PERFECT HARMONY.
- COLOSSIANS 3:12-14 -

Do you struggle with comparison, envy, or jealousy towards other women? In what ways?

In the season of mothering right now, what types of friendships do you need?

What is God speaking to you through this message today?

Prayer : Father, thank You for creating me in Your likeness. Thank You that I am not meant to do all this alone, but instead with You, my family, and a sisterhood. I ask that You will help me to reach out to others and be intentional in forming strong friendships. I pray that if there is any jealousy, or envy towards other women in my heart, that I would give that to You and begin living a life that celebrates and encourages others, lifting other women up. Help me Holy Spirit to represent You rightfully to those around me. I love You.
                                                                                                          - Amen

Check out the Trek Further section at the end of this book to apply today's lesson to your real life.

18

THANKFULNESS

It was 6 a.m. and my three-year-old stood at the side of my bed repeating over and over, *"Mommy! Mommy! Get up! I'm hungry, I want cereal!"* Before my eyes even opened, she literally coughed snot into my mouth. I quickly sat up and spat out the glob of green snot and proceeded to wipe my tongue with my shirt.

Good Lord, help me. I was cranky, irritable, all the things someone feels after being woken up with snot projected into their mouth. The day hadn't even begun and I was in a terrible mood. I stomped out of the bedroom door while throwing a pillow at my husband in efforts to wake him up and help me. He didn't even do anything wrong and I was already upset with him for not being awake.

When the day starts off like that, oh man it's hard for me to pull myself together. My mind and my feelings just want to continue in a rage of complaining and frustration, and before I know it, it's 3 p.m. and my bad attitude has tainted everything.

Please tell me I'm not the only one who easily can spiral down in feelings of irritability and frustration? I have a feeling I'm not the only one.

There is something powerful to combat waking up on the wrong side of the bed. There is something that has the influence to flip frowns upside down and turn gloomy days into sunny ones. That tool is called, thankfulness.

Thankfulness is our greatest weapon to battle a rough day.

We are always facing circumstances where we must choose to either make our bed in a pit of anger and frustration, or bring our spirit in alignment with God's character, and speak our thanks and praise. I seriously don't think anyone has to make this choice more times in a day than a mom. Honestly, with kids coughing snot into our mouths, kids pooping in the bathtub, and the full-on meltdowns in the shopping aisles, thankfulness is a serious tool we need to take hold of.

The words you speak out over your present and future situations have power. God warns us that our tongue is a sword, able to bring life or death. You create the atmosphere you live in. If you are a walking storm of anger, frustration, and complaining, you will speak that out over the circumstances you are facing. You have the choice to speak praise and thanksgiving over all unfair, unjust, and uncertain situations that come. From normal day-to-day mama struggles, to the heavy life-changing stuff, it's always our choice how we will respond.

Thankfulness has the authority to bring peace, joy, and promise into our sufferings. God says that in all things, in days when all goes well, and in days when crap hits the fan, we are to give thanks to God. We give thanks because He is worthy, and because it is the best thing for us. God knows that when we live out of thankfulness, peace and rest will rule our hearts. Through thankfulness He is able to trust us with our words and with places of leadership and authority He has given us. Mamas who choose thankfulness are mamas who hold heaven in their words and create atmospheres of peace and joy. What a powerful tool God has given us through speaking out thanksgiving.

Next time anger, worry, and frustration come knocking on your heart, choose to say, "God, I'm so thankful for the blessing of these kids. I'm so thankful that you have provided a home for us, that we have food on the table, and that there are clothes on our backs. Thank you for for this day and for life. Thank you for your goodness and for your blessings. And thank you that I have a little goober who drives me crazy sometimes, but that I have the privilege of loving and raising. You give the best gifts, Father."

REJOICE ALWAYS, PRAY WITHOUT CEASING, GIVE THANKS IN ALL
CIRCUMSTANCES; FOR THIS IS THE WILL OF GOD IN CHRIST JESUS FOR YOU.
- 1 THESSALONIANS 5:16-18 ESV -

AND WHATEVER YOU DO, IN WORD OR DEED, DO EVERYTHING IN THE NAME
OF THE LORD JESUS, GIVING THANKS TO GOD THE FATHER THROUGH HIM.
- COLOSSIANS 3:17 ESV -

I WILL GIVE THANKS TO THE LORD WITH MY WHOLE HEART;
I WILL RECOUNT ALL OF YOUR WONDERFUL DEEDS.
- PSALM 9:1 ESV -

REJOICE IN THE LORD ALWAYS; AGAIN I WILL SAY, REJOICE. LET YOUR
REASONABLENESS BE KNOWN TO EVERYONE. THE LORD IS AT HAND; DO NOT BE
ANXIOUS ABOUT ANYTHING, BUT IN EVERYTHING BY PRAYER AND SUPPLICATION
WITH THANKSGIVING LET YOUR REQUESTS BE MADE KNOWN TO GOD. AND THE PEACE
OF GOD, WHICH SURPASSES ALL UNDERSTANDING, WILL GUARD YOUR HEARTS AND
YOUR MINDS IN CHRIST JESUS.
- PHILIPPIANS 4:4-7 ESV -

I WILL GIVE TO THE LORD THE THANKS DUE TO HIS RIGHTEOUSNESS,
AND I WILL SING PRAISE TO THE NAME OF THE LORD, THE MOST HIGH.
- PSALM 7:17 ESV

THE LORD IS MY STRENGTH AND MY SHIELD; IN HIM MY HEART TRUSTS, AND I AM
HELPED; MY HEART EXULTS, AND WITH MY SONG I GIVE THANKS TO HIM.
- PSALM 28:7 ESV -

DEATH AND LIFE ARE IN THE POWER OF THE TONGUE,
AND THOSE WHO LOVE IT WILL EAT ITS FRUITS.
- PROVERBS 18:21 ESV -

When was the last time you responded to a situation in anger and frustration rather than in praise and thanksgiving?

_____
_____
_____
_____

What are you facing right now that you can speak praise and thanksgiving over?

_____
_____
_____
_____

In your own words, describe what it looks like to be a mom who lives from a place of thankfulness.

_____
_____
_____
_____

Prayer : Father, today I want to give You praise! Thank You for giving me life, thank You for Your provision, for Your blessings, for my family and children. God, no matter what I face today, and what my future holds, may I be someone who always speaks words of thankfulness in the face of all my circumstances. You are worthy of all my praise. Holy Spirit, help me to train my tongue to speak life instead of death. Help me to create spaces of peace and joy in my home and within all my relationships. I love You.

- Amen

Check out the Trek Further section at the end of this book to apply today's lesson to your real life.

Less business < More intentionality

Less striving < More slowing down

Less alone < More sisterhood

Less distracted < More present

ABUNDANCE

week four

19

A GOOD GOD

When you look back on this week, are there moments of mothering that you wish you could go back and change? Maybe you lost your cool when the kids spilled their Cheerios all over themselves, or you responded in anger after one of your kids destroyed the pile of freshly folded laundry? I for sure have moments that I can look back on this week and wish I could push the rewind button and do them over again.

We are currently remodeling our kitchen. The house is in construction mode making it hard to function normally with our two toddlers. I was feeling a bit overwhelmed this morning as I was trying to manage washing the dishes in our bedroom sink while the kids were getting into drawers they aren't allowed in and nearly running over the dishes drying on a towel below me. In the heat of the moment I shouted at them to leave the room and said something along the lines

of, *"YOU BOTH ARE MAKING IT IMPOSSIBLE TO GET ANYTHING DONE! JUST LEAVE!"* As soon as I shouted I knew I messed up. And like many times before I had to humble myself and ask my toddlers for forgiveness.

No parent is perfect. Many times, especially in the teenage years, I would argue with my parents over their curfews and dating rules. And when I was really young I was quite the fireball, I tested my parent's self-control and temper many times. Growing up, my parents were never perfect, but I never questioned if they had my best interest in mind. I never questioned if their intentions towards me were good. I could trust what they said and what they did because I knew they were good and that they loved me.

The relationship we have with our parents and our children is only a small replica of our eternal relationship with our Heavenly Father. We may not always get it right on our motherhood journey, but our Father in Heaven is always the perfect parent. When we bluntly disobey Him, He never responds in abuse. When we get angry at Him, even walk away from Him, He always meets us with grace and welcomes us back with love. When we walk through the valley of the shadow, or face unbearable circumstances, and most of all, when we are faced with things we don't understand, God is still and always a good father.

In times of trouble, we are tempted to question the core nature of who God is. The enemy comes to plant doubt in your mind by prompting the question, "But Is He really good?" And despite what we see, what we go through, and what we can't explain, the most important thing we must be able to say is that, "yes, even still, He is good."

When we choose to believe that God is good, we can trust and obey His word, because we live in the assurance of who He is. When we know God is good, we can walk through the valley of the shadow with hope of redemption and life. When we know God is good we don't doubt God's character, even when life seems to be crashing in on us. **When we know God is good, we walk with confidence into His calling and purpose for our life without fear. Fear comes when we doubt the goodness of who God is.**

Do you believe God is good? Even in the storms can you say that God is still good?

We cannot doubt the truth of His goodness as we grow in relationship with Him, and other times it's a truth we must choose to believe when we don't feel it. God has purpose and abundant life already prepared and eager to give to you. You have a good, heavenly father. His thoughts and plans are only for your good, they are only full of hope, redemption, and abundant life.

THE LORD IS MY SHEPHERD; I SHALL NOT WANT.
HE MAKES ME LIE DOWN IN GREEN PASTURES.
HE LEADS ME BESIDE STILL WATERS.
HE RESTORES MY SOUL.
HE LEADS ME IN PATHS OF RIGHTEOUSNESS
FOR HIS NAME'S SAKE.
EVEN THOUGH I WALK THROUGH THE VALLEY
OF THE SHADOW OF DEATH,
I WILL FEAR NO EVIL, FOR YOU ARE WITH ME;
YOUR ROD AND YOUR STAFF, THEY COMFORT ME.
YOU PREPARE A TABLE BEFORE ME
IN THE PRESENCE OF MY ENEMIES;
YOU ANOINT MY HEAD WITH OIL; MY CUP OVERFLOWS.
SURELY GOODNESS AND MERCY SHALL FOLLOW ME
ALL THE DAYS OF MY LIFE, AND I SHALL DWELL IN
THE HOUSE OF THE LORD FOREVER.
- PSALMS 23 ESV -

FOR I KNOW THE PLANS I HAVE FOR YOU,
DECLARES THE LORD, PLANS FOR WELFARE AND NOT
FOR EVIL, TO GIVE YOU A FUTURE AND A HOPE.
- JEREMIAH 29:11 ESV -

GIVE THANKS TO THE LORD, FOR HE IS GOOD,
FOR HIS STEADFAST LOVE ENDURES FOREVER.
- PSALMS 136:1 ESV -

What has prevented you from believing that God is good?

_____

_____

_____

_____

What is God speaking to you personally through this message?

_____

_____

_____

_____

How does knowing that the nature of God is always good change the way you live your life?

_____

_____

_____

_____

P r a y e r : Father, thank You that You are a good father. You cannot go against who You are, and that means that in all things and through all things You are good. Forgive me for ever believing the lie that You don't have good plans for me or that You don't love me. Father, would You open up my heart to receive more of Your love and experience more of Your goodness. I choose today that despite what I am facing in my life, I declare that You are a good God, and You will restore all things, and redeem all things that the enemy has meant for evil. I love You.

- Amen

Check out the Trek Further section at the end of this book to apply today's lesson to your real life.

20

SAYING YES TO THE JOURNEY

I totally used to be that teenager that would test the limits. Anyone else? Anytime there was a rule set in place I would want to question it and demand to understand why it had to be there and negotiate other options. I wanted to experience the right and the wrong to find out for myself. Needless to say, I was not your typical first born. And I see so much of myself in my oldest. Being in the midst of the toddler years, I explain the consequences of disobedience to my girls probably 100 times in one day.

Then I think of Eve, in the garden talking to a snake, knowing fully who she was and knowing fully the consequences of choosing to disobey God. Eve and Adam both knew the goodness of God, and part of His goodness was that He allowed free will, to give them a choice. His intention was always for us to have abundant life in relationship with Him, but we have to choose it. I used to get all up in arms with Eve thinking things like, "Why would you listen to a talking snake? Why didn't you just obey what God said, it's so simple!" Then I look at my life and I shout the same thing back at myself. If I believe God is good and trustworthy, then why on earth do I choose to not listen to Him?

Our flesh wants to respond to God by wanting to first experience, then make sure we feel good, and then maybe think about obeying. The problem with that mindset is that we are basing our truth and perspective on our limited experience and understanding. But God has no limitations, meaning that His knowledge is infinite, and His experience is limitless. Why would we choose to question God who has no limit to His capacity and believe we know better by our limited capacity?

God loves it when we talk with Him, and

He isn't afraid of your questions. What we need to watch out for is that we don't let our questions become accusations towards God or allow our questions to question if God is good.

We must learn to trust that God has revealed to us what we need to know and given us what we must have to fulfill what He has asked of us. Sometimes he chooses to show us the picture and gives us the paint and brush to create it, and other times He gives the paint and brush and asks us to brush stroke by stroke without knowing the outcome. Someone I respect highly said once that sometimes God doesn't tell us His plan for our life because we would kill it with disbelief. I think he's right. God in His perfect wisdom will reveal things to us in the best timing. When we hear God speak to us and we know in our hearts that He is is a good Father, we will trust and believe what he says.

I so wish I could sit there with you and talk about the things God is prompting in your heart. Maybe it's about a move, or a career change. Maybe it's about what school your kids should go to and what friends they should be around. Maybe it's about a desire placed in your heart that God has been growing and watering for some time. What is He calling you to? Maybe God has shown you the whole shebang, or maybe He is showing you the first step forward. Wherever you are in this process I want to encourage you to lean into the truth of God's goodness, and choose, like we all must, to obey what He is saying.

Through relationship with God and stepping out in obedience, the most wild and beautiful journey awaits you.

I WILL INSTRUCT YOU AND TEACH YOU IN THE WAY YOU SHOULD GO I WILL COUNSEL YOU WITH MY EYE UPON YOU. BE NOT LIKE A HORSE OR A MULE, WITHOUT UNDERSTANDING, WHICH MUST BE CURBED WITH BIT AND BRIDLE, OR IT WILL NOT STAY NEAR YOU. MANY ARE THE SORROWS OF THE WICKED, BUT STEADFAST LOVE SURROUNDS THE ONE WHO TRUSTS IN THE LORD.
- PSALMS 32:8-10 ESV -

YOU GUIDE ME WITH YOUR COUNSEL, AND AFTERWARD YOU WILL RECEIVE ME TO GLORY. WHOM HAVE I IN HEAVEN BUT YOU? AND THERE IS NOTHING ON EARTH THAT I DESIRE BESIDES YOU. MY FLESH AND MY HEART MAY FAIL, BUT GOD IS THE STRENGTH OF MY HEART AND MY PORTION FOREVER.
- PSALMS 73:24-26 ESV -

YOUR WORD IS A LAMP TO MY FEET AND A LIGHT TO MY PATH.
- PSALMS 119:105 ESV -

HEAR INSTRUCTION AND BE WISE, AND DO NOT NEGLECT IT. BLESSED IS THE ONE WHO LISTENS TO ME, WATCHING DAILY AT MY GATES, WAITING BESIDE MY DOORS.
- PROVERBS 8:33-34 ESV -

MY SHEEP HEAR MY VOICE, AND I KNOW THEM, AND THEY FOLLOW ME. I GIVE THEM ETERNAL LIFE, AND THEY WILL NEVER PERISH, AND NO ONE WILL SNATCH THEM OUT OF MY HAND.
- JOHN 10:27-28 ESV -

In your own words, write what you heard from this message?

_____

_____

_____

_____

Is there an area of your life God is asking you to obey Him in?

_____

_____

_____

_____

P r a y e r : Father, thank You for only wanting the best for me. I acknowledge that You have no limitations and that You know what is right and good. Thank You for being so personal and for Your guidance. Forgive me for times when I didn't obey You and when I chose my own desires above Your plan. Help me to learn to listen to Your voice and obey without questioning Your sovereignty. I praise You for your goodness today.

– Amen

Check out the Trek Further section at the end of this book to apply today's lesson to your real life.

21

DIE TO GAIN

SOMETIMES TO GAIN SOMETHING
PRECIOUS MEANS THAT WE HAVE
TO GIVE UP SOMETHING ELSE.

Throughout pregnancy we give up the
ability to sleep on our stomachs, but we
gain the peace of knowing our baby is
safe. In postpartum, we gain the joy of
seeing our baby's first smile, but give
up our full night sleeps. In toddlerhood,
we gain seeing their first steps and
personality come alive, but we give up hot
cups of coffee and having a real hair style.
Do you get what I'm saying? Every good
thing involves the letting go of another.
In motherhood, we give up so much, but oh
jeez do we gain more than we give.

But there's more, more treasures buried
in the deep places of our hearts, desires
and passions, dreams. What about these?
Do you ever feel guilty for wanting those
things even after being a mom? I do. Do
you ever feel like those are the things that
have been hardest to lay down in order
to gain motherhood? I do. But I believe

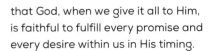

that God, when we give it all to Him, is faithful to fulfill every promise and every desire within us in His timing.

Jesus calls us into a very unconventional, backwards, upside-down life. While the whole world shouts out to focus only on yourself, Jesus says to give yourself up.

I have never experienced a greater opportunity to truly put off the old self and put on Christ than in marriage and motherhood. Every day in this journey we are given the choice to be like Jesus, to put our selfishness and fleshly desires aside and love others with the agape love of Jesus. Every day the needs of your family, the demands of parenting, the emotional and spiritual role you carry in your home and in your friendships, these things require a laying down of yourself so that others can be first.

And every day when you just want to play hide and seek with your toddler because it means that you get to hide and be alone for two seconds, God is whispering, "deny yourself, follow me, I have the grace and joy you need."

That's what's awaiting you on the other side of surrender: a life of daily bread; of grace and joy and peace for each moment in every season. Not just in parenting, but God calls us to die to ourselves in every area of life. To put off the old and put on the new. Laying down our sinful ways, laying down our emotional baggage, laying down our plans and desires and simply going to God and saying, "I'm here. I'm yours. Do all that you want in my life." And friend, this isn't a sorrowful death. This dying to self is allowing you to become who you were always meant to be. It's

dying to the false representation of you, to become who you truly are, into your true destiny since the moment God imagined you. It's a daily decision to choose to put off the old and put on Jesus, but it's a choice that leads to relationship with the Father and rich relationship with others; the whole enchilada. God isn't forcing you to choose Him, and He won't punish you for not, but He knows that when we don't live in the light, in holiness with Him, the enemy comes masked in beauty, but bearing fear and destruction.

The call Jesus brings to deny yourself and follow Him is an invitation to gain all of who He is. It is only when we lose our own self that we fully experience the power of Jesus. Being a mom reminds us of this invitation for more of Jesus. Motherhood is an opportunity to live every day in surrender, in the understanding that Jesus truly is all we need. He gives the everyday moments purpose and value. He uses all of our days to make us more like Him, to bring more of heaven everywhere we go. But to see this manifest requires we give our lives to Him.

When we see motherhood through the lenses of scripture it no longer looks routine and mundane. In the end it isn't about what we gained, but how little we become. The less we are, the greater He becomes, and if He is greater in our lives, then the life we gained will be far greater than the one we could have held on to. When we know Jesus we understand that it's all worth it. Our lives that we lay down for Him are nothing compared to the joy and hope found in Christ. The gain is unquestionably greater.

FOR TO ME TO LIVE IS CHRIST, AND TO DIE IS GAIN.
- PHILIPPIANS 1:21 ESV -

TO PUT OFF YOUR OLD SELF, WHICH BELONGS TO YOUR FORMER
MANNER OF LIFE AND IS CORRUPT THROUGH DECEITFUL DESIRES,
AND TO BE RENEWED IN THE SPIRIT OF YOUR MINDS, AND TO
PUT ON THE NEW SELF, CREATED AFTER THE LIKENESS OF GOD
IN TRUE RIGHTEOUSNESS AND HOLINESS.
- EPHESIANS 4:22-24 ESV -

What one thing in your life is God calling you to put off, and what is He calling you to put on instead?

_____

_____

_____

_____

What is a dream or desire that you have handed to God in faith that He will bring it to completion in His timing?

_____

_____

_____

_____

What else is God speaking to you through this message?

_____

_____

_____

_____

P r a y e r : Father, thank You for creating us in Your image. Thank You that You are perfect in all Your ways. Forgive me for areas of my life that I haven't lived as You have called me to live. Holy Spirit, help me to daily choose to put off the old self and put on the new. Help me to lay myself down so I can gain all of who You are. I love You.

- Amen

Check out the Trek Further section at the end of this book to apply today's lesson to your real life.

22

TRUST

We have all been there, sneaking into our newborn baby's room to check if they are still breathing. We've watched them take their first steps and then promptly begin to notice all the potential danger zones in our home. And we move mountains and drop everything to get our child to the doctor the first time we see their fever spike or we sense that something isn't right. It's part of our natural instinct as mothers to "go there" mentally and to observe danger and prevent it. The Holy Spirit, also known as our motherly instinct, is a gift from God.

But what about the bigger fears? The lie that maybe God would allow something bad to happen to your child just to test you? The fear that you're not meeting the standard emotionally and spiritually as a mom? If I'm honest, I used to fear that God would ask me do something or go somewhere because He knew I didn't want to, or even that He would cause something bad to happen to my family just to test me. The list goes on. If we search our hearts, we may see these kind of fears buried in the crevasses. What does this say about who we believe God is? Do these fears represent the God we know that is kind, good, and loving? For me, the answer was a big resounding, no!

Fear is the absence of love.

Each of us hold priceless and precious gifts in our hands, like our kids, husbands, dreams, and places. And like Peter, when Jesus called him out to the waters in the middle of a storm, Jesus was asking him, "Do you trust me? Do you believe I am who I say I am?" Peter walked on the water, but only for a moment. His doubts and fears become more of a reality than the power of Jesus. He began to sink, and as Jesus pulled him up from the water He said to Peter, "Faint-heart, what got into you?" Sister, when you doubt God, He is asking you the same. What's got into you? What fears have blinded you from His love?

Unclench your hands. Let go of the things you hold so tight to. Let them go to the one who holds all things together. Life is better when your hands are free. He is safe and kind and good. Jesus promises us that there will be valleys on this journey. He promises that sometimes storms will come, but He declares that it's okay because He has overcome it all. Nothing is exempt from the redemption of Christ. Nothing. He is the safest place to lay down your family. He is the safest place to lay down your life. When we choose to hold tightly to the people and things God has given us, He is unable to do His full work within us. And hear me, you guys, His work is *good*. His plans are good! He is not the cause of the storm. He is the safe place, the refuge, the one who holds all authority.

IMMEDIATELY HE MADE THE DISCIPLES GET INTO THE BOAT AND GO BEFORE HIM TO THE OTHER SIDE, WHILE HE DISMISSED THE CROWDS. AND AFTER HE HAD DISMISSED THE CROWDS, HE WENT UP ON THE MOUNTAIN BY HIMSELF TO PRAY. WHEN EVENING CAME, HE WAS THERE ALONE, BUT THE BOAT BY THIS TIME WAS A LONG WAY FROM THE LAND, BEATEN BY THE WAVES, FOR THE WIND WAS AGAINST THEM. AND IN THE FOURTH WATCH OF THE NIGHT HE CAME TO THEM, WALKING ON THE SEA. BUT WHEN THE DISCIPLES SAW HIM WALKING ON THE SEA, THEY WERE TERRIFIED, AND SAID, "IT IS A GHOST!" AND THEY CRIED OUT IN FEAR. BUT IMMEDIATELY JESUS SPOKE TO THEM, SAYING, "TAKE HEART; IT IS I. DO NOT BE AFRAID."
AND PETER ANSWERED HIM, "LORD, IF IT IS YOU, COMMAND ME TO COME TO YOU ON THE WATER." HE SAID, "COME." SO PETER GOT OUT OF THE BOAT AND WALKED ON THE WATER AND CAME TO JESUS. BUT WHEN HE SAW THE WIND, HE WAS AFRAID, AND BEGINNING TO SINK HE CRIED OUT, "LORD, SAVE ME." JESUS IMMEDIATELY REACHED OUT HIS HAND AND TOOK HOLD OF HIM, SAYING TO HIM, "O YOU OF LITTLE FAITH, WHY DID YOU DOUBT?" AND WHEN THEY GOT INTO THE BOAT, THE WIND CEASED. AND THOSE IN THE BOAT WORSHIPED HIM, SAYING, "TRULY YOU ARE THE SON OF GOD."
- MATTHEW 14:22-33 ESV -

THERE IS NO FEAR IN LOVE, BUT PERFECT LOVE CASTS OUT FEAR. FOR FEAR HAS TO DO WITH PUNISHMENT, AND WHOEVER FEARS HAS NOT BEEN PERFECTED IN LOVE.
- 1 JOHN 4:18 ESV -

What area of your life are you holding on to that God is asking you to trust Him with?

_____

_____

_____

What fears stop you from fully trusting God?

_____

_____

_____

Write a prayer to God laying down those fears.

_____

_____

_____

_____

Prayer : Father, I thank You because You are the one and true safe place for me. Thank You that You are completely trustworthy and deserving of my whole heart. Holy Spirit, today will You help me to walk away from my fears and into the promises and kindness of Jesus. I choose to open my hands and let go of the things holding me back from embracing abundant life in You. I trust You, and I choose today to walk in that trust.

- Amen

Check out the Trek Further section at the end of this book to apply today's lesson to your real life.

23

HAND IT OVER

Our first year of marriage was rough.

Months after our wedding Josh and I faced some serious hardships. Our communication was poor, we both became quite selfish, and forms of betrayal entered and trust began to break. As the rebuilding of trust commenced, I found myself overwhelmed with unforgiveness and unrest. I felt like every day I was spiraling downward into a pit of anxiety, and I was emotionally teeter-tottering throughout the day.

I knew something had to change, but I didn't know how or when. But Jesus spoke to me one night as I sat in the doorway of our apartment at 1:00 a.m. He said, "Lexi, I will rebuild this marriage, if you allow me to take it. Josh will disappoint you, and you will need to forgive again. The only one who will never disappoint you, will never hurt you, and will never fail to protect you, is me. Give it all to me." Cue the water works. I melted right there on the floor. I sat up from my seat, feeling like a zombie physically, but alive in my heart. Jesus, the taker and fixer of my burdens, was calling me to give it all to him.

The Father didn't send His son so that you can carry all your anxieties and pain around with you. He has no limitations and there is no end to His capacity to take and redeem all broken things. His desire for you is to give Him the emotional pain you have, to hand over to Him the injustice that was done to you, and to free yourself from the bondage of these things. We cannot control what has been done to us, but we are responsible for what we do with it. Will we hold on to pain and control, bearing the weight of it until it crashes in on us, or will be surrender it to Jesus?

Here's the hard truth - we are messy, feeling, humans. And life is messy, too. Something

we struggle to talk about as Christians is that following Christ does not mean a easier life. It does not mean things are fair. And it certainly doesn't mean we won't suffer. What it does mean is that we carry hope in the middle of the mess. And it means that we have someone who carries our burdens for us. Suffering and peace can coexist, so can suffering and joy. Have you ever experienced the two emotions working simutaiously in you? That's Jesus working in you right smack dab in the middle of the storm. Friend, I wish I could say that a life with Christ means that you are exempt from suffering, but that isn't true. We will go through hard things, maybe it's losing a job, maybe it's abuse, maybe it's the loss of a child. Your stronghold is Jesus, He carries your burdens, He extends you grace, He brings the peace, and He is your hope.

But fear cannot coexist in our suffering. Fear is not allowed in any area of our life and was never meant to be something we carry as followers of Christ. Jesus says to us, "I have told you these things, so that in me you may have peace. In this world you will have trouble. Fear not! I have overcome the world."
-John 16:33

Rest and peace are fruits of abundant life. When we choose to give our burdens to Jesus, He in turn gives us His rest. When we say to God, the weight of what I'm experiencing is too heavy, what I'm feeling is too much for me to carry, I don't understand what's happening, will you take it Father and replace it with your peace? In our releasing, He is able to do His good work. He says that He is kind and gentle in heart, and through Him we will find rest for our souls. This is abundant life in Christ. Not that life is easy or that we never walk through the dark valleys, but that He is there to exchange our burdens for rest. He is gentle and humble in heart; He is there to free you from your burdens.

COME TO ME, ALL WHO LABOR AND ARE HEAVY LADEN,
AND I WILL GIVE YOU REST. TAKE MY YOKE UPON YOU,
AND LEARN FROM ME, FOR I AM GENTLE AND LOWLY
IN HEART, AND YOU WILL FIND REST FOR YOUR SOULS.
FOR MY YOKE IS EASY, AND MY BURDEN IS LIGHT.
- MATTHEW 11:28-30 ESV -

HUMBLE YOURSELVES, THEREFORE, UNDER THE MIGHTY
HAND OF GOD SO THAT AT THE PROPER TIME HE MAY
EXALT YOU, CASTING ALL YOUR ANXIETIES ON HIM,
BECAUSE HE CARES FOR YOU.
- 1 PETER 5:6-7 ESV -

What is God speaking to you through this message?

Is there a burden you feel like He is asking you to give to Him?

How will you respond to Jesus with your burdens today?

Prayer : Father, I thank You because You care so deeply about my heart. I thank You because You are kind and gentle hearted. Father, You are so good. Forgive me for the things in my life that I have not released to You. Forgive me for holding onto worry and anxiety when You already made a way for all things to be redeemed. Holy Spirit, help me today to begin releasing all my burdens unto the Lord. I know healing is a process, and I choose to begin that process with You today. I love You.

- Amen

Check out the Trek Further section at the end of this book to apply today's lesson to your real life.

24

FREEDOM
IN CHRIST

I want to give you a big hug and a high five, because you, my friend, have almost completed this whole devotional. For a mama, this is quite the accomplishment, and I'm proud. Jesus is so good, right? Spending time with Him fills us, restores us, comforts us. We are both on this journey, and I want to cheer you on as you follow Jesus, our True North, the Way to the Father.

Freedom in Christ is living a life free of fear. It's a life of turning from the old self and walking more and more into its intended identity. It's a life that leans into God's goodness and not into its own understanding. Freedom is abundant life.

Abundant life is yours, mama. Jesus died to restore relationship between you and the Father. You have been created in the image and likeness of Christ, you have been given the tools of grace, wisdom, and love to live life well, and you have been given the choice to walk in obedience and surrender it all to a good God. This is the journey to life, to a life of freedom.

God promises that in Him and only in Him you can have abundant and eternal life. He promises that in the midst of childbearing years, of making tiny and big disciples, of learning what it means to be a wife, He is Emmanuel and El Roi, the God who is with you and sees you. He has set a destiny before you that you can trust Him with. He has come to redeem and make new all things broken.

You are already loved. You are already enough.

You are a home to the living God! And where the Spirit of the Lord is, there is freedom! Mama, you are free from sin, free from burdens, free from the old, and you have been clothed in the new.

The freedom we received in Christ should propel us to go and love wildly. Because we love Jesus, because He is so, so good, we step into motherhood with a mandate and purpose, to love Father, Son, and Spirit with all of ourselves, and to love our little ones, our husbands, and all others with the agape love of Jesus.

Motherhood isn't over, yet. Jesus will continue to guide you on the destiny He has in store for you, deeper and deeper into relationship with Him. We will mess up, we will have to remember over and over again, but Jesus will stay good and faithful through the process. I pray that as you keep running this path of motherhood that you would fall more in love with Jesus, our greatest friend. Through God's grace, you've got this mama!

NOW THE LORD IS THE SPIRIT, AND WHERE
THE SPIRIT OF THE LORD IS, THERE IS FREEDOM.
-2 CORINTHIANS 3:17 ESV -

FOR YOU WERE CALLED TO FREEDOM, BROTHERS.
ONLY DO NOT USE YOUR FREEDOM AS AN OPPORTUNITY
FOR THE FLESH, BUT THROUGH LOVE SERVE ONE ANOTHER.
FOR THE WHOLE LAW IS FULFILLED IN ONE WORD:
"YOU SHALL LOVE YOUR NEIGHBOR AS YOURSELF."
- GALATIANS 5:13-14 ESV -

FOR FREEDOM CHRIST HAS SET US FREE;
STAND FIRM THEREFORE, AND DO NOT SUBMIT
AGAIN TO A YOKE OF SLAVERY.
- GALATIANS 5:1 ESV -

Imagine living your life in the fullness and freedom that Jesus offers.
How would your life look different? What does that life look like for you?

What is God speaking to you through this message? And how will you respond?

Prayer : To close, write your own prayer to God below.

Closing Blessing: May the Lord bless you and keep you. May the Lord make His face shine upon you and be gracious to you. May the Lord lift His countenance upon you and give you peace.

– Numbers 6:24-26 ESV

Check out the Trek Further section at the end of this book to apply today's lesson to your real life.

You are in relationship with a good, good God. As you say "yes" to His ways, you walk into a life of abundance. As you hand over your fears, trust who He is, and boldly walk the path He is showing you, you become a mama of freedom, a mama who brings the kingdom of God to earth.

TREK FURTHER

Hey sis! Want to take each day of this devotional even deeper?
This Trek Further section offers practical advice targeted to help
you apply what you have read to your real life. This section will
be helpful if you're reading through this study on your own, or a
great tool to walk through together with a small group. Enjoy!

True North - Day 1

Today I challenge you to write the words "True North" on your hand, and when you see it think these words, "Jesus, you are the Way, the Truth, and the Life, and I choose you today."

Holy Spirit: Our Helper - Day 2

Holy Spirit is your ultimate counselor and helper in parenting. He knows everything you need to know about raising little ones, and He's there to help you do it. As followers of Jesus we are not following a religion, but we are pursuing relationship with God. That means that God's Spirit is ready to talk to us, lead us, and make more of God known to us. Inviting the Holy Spirit into our journey of motherhood means that we can actively hear His voice and receive His guidance. Let's do an exercise together! Grab a piece of paper and pen and follow the steps below.

1. What area do you need the guidance of the Holy Spirit right now? It can be what you wrote in the processing questions of this day or something different. Maybe it's in parenting or maybe it's an issue your facing in your marriage.

    Write it down.

2. Take a few minutes in silence. Ask the Holy Spirit to bring you wisdom in what steps to take in this situation. Give time to listen to His voice and write down what He says. If you have never heard God's voice before, don't worry, neither have I! I'm not talking about the audible voice of God. People have experienced hearing the audible voice of God, but more often when God speaks to us it comes in different forms. When Holy Spirit speaks it can feel like a strong impression towards an action you should take. Or maybe He gives you a picture in your mind that will help you know what He is speaking. Maybe a specific scripture will come to mind that the Holy Spirit wants to guide you through. He is limitless in the ways He engages with us, and it can be different with everyone.

    It also takes practice. Hearing God's voice is like exercising a new muscle. It takes practice to recognize the voice of God when our own inner voice and voices of others can interfere. If you find it hard to point out God's voice, then I would suggest spending time in His presence. The more we know someone the easier it is to recognize their character, the way they communicate, what is in their nature, and what isn't. Pursuing a relationship with God will bring us closer to knowing His voice.

    John 10:27- My sheep hear my voice, and I know them, and they follow me.

3. Take time to listen and write down any impression, picture, or word you felt the Holy Spirit sharing with you about the challenge you are facing.

I hope you can take this tool of hearing God's voice and apply it to your every day. Don't be discouraged in this process, keep spending time knowing the Father, and invite others to pray with you.

But First, Jesus - Day 3

What happened on the cross was powerful. Powerful enough to change your life for eternity, and to change the struggles you face right now. Our culture today has romanticized the idea of needing superficial things to "get through" the day. We turn to social media to turn off our brain while we scroll, and we feed our desire to be known by our "likes" and "re-tweets." When used in the wrong way, for the wrong reason, even good things can create distance between us and God. Next time you find yourself turning to something to fill a void, remember the name of your friend, Jesus. Start by telling Him all about it. Tell Him what hurts, what isn't fair, what you're feeling good about, and sad about. Tell Him what you need, and ask Him to be your main source of life. He says in His Word that when we seek Him we will find Him. Seek Him, first.

H.O.M.E - Day 4

Sometimes actively applying spiritual growth to our lives is easier said than done. To help increase awareness of the Holy Spirit in your life, choose at least one practice below and make a commitment to work on doing it daily.

Take the challenge of speaking this over yourself each morning, "the Holy Spirit is alive and working inside of me now, and every day. I am a home for the Holy Spirit, and through Christ I am being made more like Him each day. I am one with my heavenly Father, I am made new in Christ, and I have an everlasting relationship with God."

Take note in your journal or in your phone when you hear the Holy Spirit speaking to you in small or big ways.

You are one with the Spirit of God, which means that you are able to speak with Him everywhere and in every situation. Challenge yourself to speak with God throughout your day.

Baptized with Christ - Day 5

The death and resurrection of Jesus on the cross gave us the choice to also walk in that death and resurrection. This means that when we choose to follow Jesus we begin living life under the umbrella of love and grace, not of rigorous rules and shame. I want to encourage you to do two things.

1. If you have made the decision to follow Jesus and haven't been baptized, maybe

the perfect time is now. Baptism is a symbolic action of us dying to sin as Christ did, and then coming out of the water, cleansed, and in the resurrection life with Christ. Our Spirit comes alive and awake in new ways when we share publicly our faith in Christ and actively support that decision with baptism. If you're reading through this study with a small group, share openly together if you have been baptized, what it meant for you, what you feel God is speaking to you personally about baptism.

2. Take a moment and ask the Holy Spirit if you are still holding on to anything that He has already paid the price for. Too often we carry around a metaphorical "shame purse" that we keep hidden from others. I encourage you to get that purse out, dump its contents on the table and sort it out. Get with a girlfriend, talk to your tribe, gather around people who will pray with you to help you release something that you have held on to that Jesus has already paid the price for.

Don't steal back what God paid for. It doesn't belong to you. From now on, every morning when you wake up and you walk under your door frame, imagine it says in big bold beautiful letters, "Love and Grace." You my friend, live under perfect love and abundant grace.

Jesus Today and Always - Day 6

This is the most important thing: to know that Jesus came to complete one amazing goal, and that was to restore you to the Father. Jesus came to share God's love with you, for you to become one with Him, and then compel you to share His love with others. Today that message is still very much alive and true. Every day is another day that the gospel is being told to the world, and every day we have the choice to seek first His kingdom and pursue our relationship with Jesus before any other pursuit. This is why we were created, and it is the only thing that will satisfy and last forever.

With that being said, rest assured that "quiet time" is going to look a whole lot different sometimes in this season of mothering, and that's totally okay. If you're finding time to read through this study, then you deserve a big fist bump. I have listed a few ways to spend time with Jesus even when life is messy.

During house cleaning, meal preparing, or even on the go, look up YouTube videos or download podcasts of sermons that inspire you. In my home I often have a video study being played that I can listen to while I'm doing all the other things. When something hits my spirit, I pull out my phone and quickly write it down to meditate on later.

If your kids are in school, commit to dedicating an hour of your time, one or two days a week with Jesus before getting to the errands. There will always be more laundry, more work, but sometimes saying, "but first, Jesus" is something we need to learn.

During tasks like, dishwashing, driving, showering, or even going to the bathroom (I'm serious), be intentional to pray and just speak to God. Allowing God into the moments of your day forms a reminder that He is constant and always ready to speak with you. Some of the moments I have felt the closest to God have been over a sink full of dishes!

Image Bearer - Day 7

Just to recap: firstly, you were created to be in relationship with God. Secondly, throughout this life you will wear many hats, all of which hold responsibility and purpose for kingdom benefit. Thirdly, you were created in the image of God. Because of who He is, you are. Choose a few areas that you struggle with seeing how God sees you and find a verse that speaks the truth of how God sees you. For example, I struggle with speaking in front of people, but I feel God wants to challenge me in this. After this verse in Matthew I realised that on my own maybe I won't be able to face my fear of public speaking, but because God is able to do all these, I can also do this with Him. "But Jesus looked at them and said, "with man this is impossible, but with God all things are possible."" Matthew 19:26 ESV

Seen - Day 8

Start a "I'm With you" journal. This looks like getting a small notepad or maybe starting a "Note" on your phone and begin documenting all the moments throughout the day that God reminds you that He's present. I'm serious, you guys, this is important. So many times God is reminding us that He is with us and we have closed our eyes to see it. Ask God to remind you throughout the day and He will. Changing a diaper at midnight and you remember that Jesus is with you, write it down. In the middle of errands and you are reminded, "Hey, I'm here, I'm always here." Write it down. Maybe it's something you see or a gift that you're randomly given that you feel God had part in to remind you that you're not alone, write it down. Practicing awareness of God's presence will begin to make us sensitive to seeing and experiencing Him more.

Confident - Day 9

Testimonies, testimonies, testimonies! The most efficient way to build confidence is God's faithfulness is to hear people share testimonies of God's faithfulness. Testimonies build us up, they spur on hope, and they help us look towards God. When I'm feeling a little low in the confidence department of my faith, I find podcasts that talk about God's faithfulness, or I reach out and ask a friend to share a story of how God has shown up in their life. We need to hear these stories. Surrounding our heart and filling our mind with testimonies like this will provoke our Spirit to rest in confidence in God.

Grace-full - Day 10

When we choose to act out of what we believe, instead of what we feel, that will dramatically change the way we live. Next time, when you're faced with a situation that feels overwhelming, and you feel hopeless, tired, angry, (fill in your emotion here) name the truth of who God is and who you are in Him. For example, you are up for the seventh time in one night because your baby won't sleep. You're feeling irritable, tired, just totally over it. Pray something like this: "God, here's how I feel. I know that you are full of grace, and therefore, because you live within me, I can tap into that grace at any moment. Would you give me the grace to love my child well tonight? Would you fill me with what I need to respond to my baby, my husband, and myself in love?" Friend, He can, and He will, do it. We don't have to live by our feelings, we live life from a new standpoint.

Loved - Day 11

Jesus says that others will know we are His disciples by the way we love. It starts with knowing that we are loved first. So many of us struggle sealing this truth into our identity. Let me be straight with you - God's word says you are loved, period. What God says is always the final word. We all have brokenness in our lives, and we all are discovering the love of Christ through our own journey. I would encourage you to dig into the gospels. If you don't know which one to start in, I would suggest the Gospel of John. Jesus shows us the love of God through every moment recorded of His life.

Another practical thing that may be helpful is asking God throughout the day what He thinks of you. Does this sound silly? He loves you. He wants to tell you that in His own way. So ask Him, give Him space to speak truth over you, and allow it to gradually change your own understanding.

I Am Mama, Hear Me Roar - Day 12

Okay, mama, I want you to dream big for a bit. Being made to be in relationship with God, and carrying His image is a beautiful gift. Now let's take it a step further, you have been given a set of giftings and dreams by the Father that are to express His love to the world. What are your dreams? What puts a fire in your belly? What do you do without having to be told to do it? What comes naturally to you? What brings you life? My guess is that whatever popped in your mind while reading those questions was placed there for a purpose by God. So sister, take time to write those things down. Get them on paper and take a look at them. Start talking with God about how these things can begin to manifest in your life, big or small. God cares about seasons of life and He can place vision in your heart weeks, months, or years before He wants you to pursue that vision. But bringing those desires that He has given you back to Him in prayer will begin the process of discovering when and how to step into those giftings.

The Magic Word - Day 13

Maybe you want to get back to the things that matter, and have time for the people and the assignments that God has asked you to steward well, but you just don't know where to start. The good news is that we don't have to do this on our own. We can chat with God about this and ask Him for His wisdom and direction for our lives. He cares about how you use your time and energy, and He is willing and waiting to help guide you to the right way.

Ask yourself this question:
What has God given me and asked me to steward well, and what is in my way of doing that?

Legacy - Day 14

A helpful tool in cultivating a healthy home life is finding families that you look up to. Take a look around you and find a few families who do life well together. Reach out and ask them what they value as a family, what habits they have implemented in their home life that have made a positive impact. Looking at families that are a few steps ahead in raising kids or in seasons of life is a rich gift that we should press into.

Love Yourself - Day 15

It's easy to get discouraged when you make a plan to invest in your own needs and then life just takes over. Start small and make attainable goals. In the section below list two things you can do this week that are attainable and life-giving to you. For example: plan a child-free coffee date with a friend, go get a fresh new haircut, or spend an evening after the kids are in bed to start a new book instead of cleaning up.

Most importantly, you must give yourself permission. If self-care isn't something you are used to, it can feel strange and selfish. Start with permission, sign the agreement below to commit to yourself that you will begin loving yourself in new ways.

I, _____ , give myself permission to think of my own needs. I choose to make time to nourish my mind, body, and soul this week.

This week I will _____

_____

_____

_____

Love Your Man - Day 16

Sometimes it's hard to know where to start when you are intentionally growing your marriage. Instead of doing all the right things, just begin with being intentional in the way you love. Here are four things you can start doing now to water the covenant relationship with your husband.

Schedule a date night twice a month. Have it on the calendar, set up the babysitter, make it happen.

Sometimes we love our husbands the way we want to be loved, and in reality they feel loved in different ways than us. Talk to each other about what makes you feel loved, and make it a goal to once a day love your husband in his love language. For years I would cook Josh a nice meal, spend quality time with him, and even buy him gifts … but he still didn't feel loved by me. It wasn't until I understood that he felt most loved when I would hug him, rub his back, and speak words of encouragement to him.

There's nothing wrong with scheduling sex. There's not. Frankly, sex isn't always spontaneous, and often after having kids it takes a whole lot of intentionality. We make time for what's important, and intimacy in relationship will increase your emotional unity. Maybe give it a try?

Make a commitment to attend one marriage retreat, marriage course, or marriage conference every year together. Be proactive in building a strong and healthy marriage. Be preventative, instead of trying to make up for it when things begin to spiral down.

Sisterhood in Motherhood – Day 17

Do you have a sisterhood? If not, make it a goal and prayer point for your life. The good news is that because relationships are important to God, He will show you the people to seek after. Maybe it will be just two or three women, but it doesn't need to be a whole lot. Ask God to bring to mind women you know that you can intentionally reach out to, or ask Him to bring new people into your life. The trick is being brave. Nurturing friendships, being vulnerable, and allowing certain people to have a place to speak into your life takes trust and stepping out. Just like every good and life-giving thing in this world, it will take work and intention. So, be brave, step out, and choose to live life closely with others.

Who are three women that you can encourage and bless this week? And how?

List two or three names of women you would like to intentionally invest more time in, in the coming weeks. Maybe schedule a "mama and baby" coffee meet up each week, a Bible study group, or set up a time to visit each other's homes. You, girlfriend, are capable of being a leader.

Thankfulness - Day 18

Shifting our mind and spirit to the path of thankfulness can be challenging depending on what we are walking through. I want to encourage you to carry a small journal with you for one week. In this journal, write down everything you are thankful for throughout your day. If you're finding it hard to love someone in your life right now, ask God to help you write down all the things you are thankful for about that person. If you're facing something that is flooding you with worry and stress, write out thanksgiving for God's faithfulness and goodness over that situation. God says to rejoice always and give thanks through all circumstances. Speak out praise and thanksgiving as an act of spiritual warfare over your life, in all areas, big and small.

A Good God - Day 19

We live in a broken world, with broken people, and broken fathers and mothers. Not everyone has grown up knowing that they can trust their parents. If your image of God has been tainted by your relationship with your earthly parents, then this helpful tip is for you.

There is so much to be said and processed on this subject, and these short paragraphs won't allow for everything that can be said. Sometimes for our relationship with God to be restored or to go deeper, we must forgive our earthly fathers and mothers, and also distinguish our earthly parents from our heavenly father.

I would encourage you to find someone you trust to walk you through this process and pray for you. Choosing to forgive our parents for the hurt and influence they have made in our lives doesn't mean forgetting the past and restoring a relationship. Sometimes yes, but in some situations this would be unhealthy. Having wise mentors in your life that can help guide you through that process is important. Forgiving others is a vital step in setting yourself free from what they have done to you and restoring the true image of your heavenly father.

Secondly, with the help of other believers and the Holy Spirit, ask God to show you His Father heart. Ask Him to renew your image of Him, not based on your personal experience, but based on who God is. Maybe this means to start by writing down all the characteristics of God found in scripture, or meditating on Psalms 23, allowing God's heart to settle into yours.

Because I know God is good, I know He wants to restore all areas of your heart, and He wants to reveal who He is to you.

Saying Yes to the Journey - Day 20

If you just read this and you're like, "But wait a minute, hold up, nah, you don't know what God is asking me. It's too much, it's too hard, so yeah, no, I'll pass." If that's you, then okay. It's a choice to obey God, remember. No one is forcing you. My question for you would be, what fears are in between God's best for you and your hesitation? Fear and unbelief can prevent us from stepping into obedience to God, because we say things like, "but I can't do it, I'm not good enough, but I would have to give up that or stop doing that". If those phrases come to mind, then remember that it is only by God's grace we can do what He calls us to, and that God only has the highest plans for us. Talk to God about it. Lay it all out.

I believe hearing and obeying is so important in motherhood. There are so many moments, big and small, where we have the choice to obey God in our parenting journeys. These crazy, wonderful kids of yours are under your stewardship until adulthood, and seeking God in areas of schooling, friendships, and activities is part of your role as a parent.

A short story. When searching for babysitters for my kids there was one time when God spoke clearly to me not to leave my kids alone with someone. I had no reason to believe anything bad of this person, in fact, I loved them dearly and respected them. From my experience and my perspective, there was nothing to cause concern. But, God spoke clearly, and I knew I had the choice to hear and obey or to go off my limited understanding. I decided to listen. I still don't have reason to believe this person wasn't trustworthy, but I knew I made the right call that day.

Obeying God means not being distracted by our own perspectives. I encourage you to not base decisions only on what other people say or how things look, but first seek God in parenting decisions. God will speak to your spirit when something isn't right, or nudge you in the right direction when choices have to be made.

Die to Gain - Day 21

We are all on the journey to becoming our true selves again, back to who God created us to be. This process takes a whole lot of renewing of our mind. We daily need to ask Holy Spirit to help us put off things like anger, jealousy, bitterness, pride, just to name a few. The Word says to be transformed by the renewing of our mind. Today, pick one verse from the Bible that will encourage you to put on who you are in Christ, and place it where you will see it. Write it on a sticky note and place it in your car, set it as the lock screen on your phone, or maybe place it in the diaper drawer, somewhere you will consistently be reminded.

For example, if I want to put off my fleshly response to become angry with my kids, and put on the attitude and actions of Christ, I could write the verse from Psalm 103:8,

"The Lord is compassionate and gracious, slow to anger, abounding in love." When I feel anger rising within me, I can stop and remember this verse, and ask Holy Spirit to help me be slow to anger, gracious, and loving. Putting off the old and putting on Christ.

Trust - Day 22

Trusting God is more than just a thing we say. We can't say that we trust God if we are not able to actively walk out that trust. I want to encourage you to not only declare that you trust God with your family, your finances, your life path, but to walk that trust out in action. This means not complaining to others about your fears or hardships, but speak out the promises of God even in the storms. This looks like letting go of overbearing control within your marriage and choosing to trust that God is in control. Even in the storms, may your actions back up your words.

Find for yourself a couple scriptures that you can go back to when you need to put your trust in God. Repeating these and meditating on them helps to reroute your fears back into alignment with God.

Hand it Over - Day 23

When Josh and I were rebuilding the trust in our marriage, God showed me a simple way to release my worries to Him. This exercise might feel silly, but I did it every day, sometimes 50 times a day until soon enough I wasn't doing it anymore. This is serious business when it comes to our souls, so if you need to do this while shopping in Target (I did!) or in the drive-through line, or at home in the middle of dish washing, do it, friend.

Here it goes. Hold your hands out in front of you like you are carrying something. Think of what it is you are worried about, or the fear you have, or the pain you are facing. Don't shove it behind you, but allow it to come forward and name it. Then pretend like you are putting that thing in your hands, and then slowly lift your hands up towards heaven and release it to Jesus.

We don't want to shove away our pain, we want to give it away. This doesn't mean all pain and worry will always go away right then and there. By starting a habit of giving our burdens to Jesus, we start on a path of healing and redemption.

Freedom in Christ - Day 24

Like I said, if you set aside time to read through this book and invest in your relationship with God, and you're a mom, and you actually completed it, well done!

Personally, I get very few things completed these days raising kids, so I don't want to pretend like this isn't a victory in it's self.

Today I would love for you to take time to reflect. If you're doing this study on your own, then write down three main points that God highlighted to you throughout these 24 days of going deeper with Him. What struck your Spirit in a fresh way? What will be your top three take-a-ways from this book?

If you've been going through this book with a group of friends I want you to do the same thing, but share your three main take-a-ways with each other, and then pray for one another.

Reflecting on what God has done in us is so important. Writing down revelations, new understanding, and words you feel God speaking to you allows you to look back and remember what God has done. Remembering what God has done helps us to be reminded of His faithfulness and His goodness.

Well done, mama!

Hi there!

I hope this devotional was a helpful tool in enhancing your relationship with God, rooting yourself in your true identity, and a reminder that you are part of a motherhood that is cheering you on. If you have any questions, comments, or want to simply reach out and chat, you can find me on Instagram at "Lexinorell", or email me at, lexinorell@gmail.com.

I hope to hear from you,

Lexi

Lightning Source UK Ltd.
Milton Keynes UK
UKHW051557100919
349488UK00009B/137/P